DEREGULATION AND AIRLINE COMPETITION

ORGANISATION FOR ECONOMIC CO-OPERATION AND DEVELOPMENT

Pursuant to article 1 of the Convention signed in Paris on 14th December, 1960, and which came into force on 30th September, 1961, the Organisation for Economic Co-operation and Development (OECD) shall promote policies designed:

- to achieve the highest sustainable economic growth and employment and a rising standard of living in Member countries, while maintaining financial stability, and thus to contribute to the development of the world economy;
- to contribute to sound economic expansion in Member as well as non-member countries in the process of economic development; and
- to contribute to the expansion of world trade on a multilateral, non-discriminatory basis in accordance with international obligations.

The original Member countries of the OECD are Austria, Belgium, Canada, Denmark, France, the Federal Republic of Germany, Greece, Iceland, Ireland, Italy, Luxembourg, the Netherlands, Norway, Portugal, Spain, Sweden, Switzerland, Turkey, the United Kingdom and the United States. The following countries acceded subsequently through accession at the dates hereafter: Japan (28th April, 1964), Finland (28th January, 1969), Australia (7th June, 1971) and New Zealand (29th May, 1973).

The Socialist Federal Republic of Yugoslavia takes part in some of the work of the OECD (agreement of 28th October, 1961).

Publié en français sous le titre:

DÉRÉGLEMENTATION ET CONCURRENCE
DANS LE TRANSPORT AÉRIEN

This report forms part of the project on competition policy and deregulation undertaken by the Committee on Competition Law and Policy. It has been based mainly on replies to a questionnaire received from 17 Member countries - Australia, Denmark, Finland, France, Germany, Greece, Ireland, Japan, Netherlands, New Zealand, Norway, Portugal, Spain, Sweden, Switzerland, the United Kingdom and the United States, two country studies concerning Canada and the United States - as well as on information supplied by the Commission of the European Communities and on available economic literature. It also draws on consultants' reports on experience with deregulation measures in the United Kingdom and the United States as well as a study of the impact of computer reservation systems on competition. The report was approved by the Committee on Competition Law and Policy in February 1988 and the OECD Council agreed to its derestriction on 21st April 1988. The three consultants' reports have been derestricted by the Secretary-General on the understanding that they remain under the responsibility of their authors.

TABLE OF CONTENTS

A. INTRODUCTION AND SUMMARY

1.   Passenger air transport is a major activity in all OECD countries. It is an industry subject to extensive regulation at the national and international level which profoundly limits competition in the sector. The most important national constraint is the need to obtain a licence to operate which usually specifies the routes to be operated, the level of capacity that may be offered as well as the fares that may be put into effect. In the United States, however, since deregulation no such restrictions are placed on air carriers and a certificate to engage in air transport is awarded to any US person who is fit, willing and able. Certain other countries have also begun to liberalise the conditions for awarding operating licences.

2.   International air transport is regulated by a complex network of bilateral and multilateral government agreements and International Air Transport Association (IATA) rules based on the Chicago Convention of 1944. The bilateral agreements vary in their form but generally specify the services and routes to be operated between the two countries, designate the airlines to operate the services and the capacity to be provided by each airline and specify the conditions under which passengers may be taken or picked up in each country and flown to third countries (so-called fifth freedom rights). Cabotage (foreign carriers operating on domestic routes) is seldom provided for. Fares are usually agreed between the airlines themselves through IATA and need to be approved by both Governments.

3.   The industry is segmented into two parts: scheduled and non-scheduled (charter), though the dividing line is becoming increasingly difficult to draw. The non-scheduled market is significant in Europe, accounting for about a quarter of the total number of passengers carried and over 55 per cent in terms of passenger kilometres in 1985. It may however decrease in importance as liberalisation of scheduled services increases. In Japan and the United States, the amount of non-scheduled traffic is negligible. Non-scheduled services are free of most of the restrictions applied to scheduled services. Travel on such services has often been subject to the conditions that the aircraft operator not sell tickets individually or directly to the public, that the tickets be part of an overall package (including accommodation or other facility) and that there be a minimum and/or maximum length of stay. However, in recent years there has been an increase in the number of "seat-only" charters.

4.   The public service nature of air transport, ensuring a regular and reliable provision of air services to all parts of a country at the lowest cost consistent with a reasonable return to carriers, has been advanced as the principal reason for national regulation of entry, capacity and fares. This argument has been put forward particularly in OECD countries with domestic markets which are considered too small to support competition and which therefore require continued detailed regulation and/or public ownership of the national airline.

5.   The major effects of regulation are that airlines are restricted from entering particular national and international markets. The level of output of an airline, when it is allowed to operate a particular route, is not at its own discretion but is often limited by capacity agreements laid down in bilateral agreements or through inter-airline agreements on revenue sharing. Pricing freedom has also been substantially restricted by IATA conferences or by governments at both ends of a particular route, though recent developments on North Atlantic and Asian routes and on certain European routes have introduced greater pricing flexibility. High tariffs have also encouraged the growth of low fare charters at the expense of scheduled services. The wide variation in fares on routes which are outwardly similar suggests that there is considerable cross-subsidization between routes and between different classes of passengers on the same route.

6.   In Europe, inter-airline pooling agreements have been the commercial arrangements by which the bilateral government agreements are put into effect. According to the 1982 European Civil Aviation Conference's COMPAS report, some 93 per cent of intra-European bilateral agreements had capacity provisions. The pooling arrangements between two airlines almost always cover revenue sharing, mostly with limitations or a ceiling (often of the order of 1 to 5 per cent) of the amount of revenue to be shared.

7.   Apart from being restricted by regulation of entry to a particular route, competition among airlines is also constrained by the physical limitations on the number of slots and gates available at airports. The question of access to scarce airport facilities, particularly gates and slots, has become a significant issue at several crowded airports, especially in the United States following deregulation, and is likely to become crucial as liberalisation proceeds in Europe and elsewhere. In general current practice gives encumbent airlines perpetual rights to airport slots ("grandfather rights") which can create a significant barrier to entry for new airlines. However, in the United States airport slots are initially allocated by the Federal Aviation Administration and a free market has been created for the buying and selling of slots between airlines, whereas in Europe unused slots or slots which have become vacant are usually allocated in the final analysis by airport scheduling committees according to IATA guidelines.

8.   Due to the extensive national and international regulations, the air transport sector is subject to some degree of exemption from national competition laws in most OECD countries. Most commonly these exemptions exist for agreements between carriers relating to government approved tariffs, schedules and other operating conditions. On the other hand, mergers between airlines or abuses of dominant position by airlines are usually subject to control under competition laws, even though this control may sometimes be exercised jointly by the competition and aviation authorities.

9.   In recent years, the restrictions placed on competition in air transport have been increasingly viewed as inimical to consumer and carrier interests in many OECD countries. Following airline deregulation in the US which began in 1978, many other OECD countries have begun to review national regulations of the passenger air transport sector and some have taken measures to liberalise the systems in operation. In the United States, there is strong evidence that deregulation has been generally beneficial, while in the United Kingdom, the partial deregulation of domestic air transport and the liberalisation of the new bilateral agreement between the Netherlands and the

United Kingdom which came into effect in 1984 appear to have brought some benefits in the form of increased traffic and lower fares.

10.   Liberalisation of bilateral agreements between countries would seem to be an essential first step towards lowering international air fares. As regards Europe, the liberalisation package adopted on December 14th by the Council of Transport Ministers of the European Communities which came into effect on 1st January 1988 should help establish greater flexibility in fares and capacity sharing as well as promoting more direct flights between small regional airports and capitals.

11.   It has been argued that airline deregulation in the United States has led to a decrease in safety standards due to cost-cutting by airlines to gain a competitive advantage. This report finds no empirical evidence in support of this view. On the contrary, the average accident rate has declined since 1978. In addition, the Federal Aviation Administration in the US continues to regulate air safety and has not allowed a reduction in safety standards since economic deregulation. The appropriate response to any real defects in safety standards would appear to be to increase safety standards or improve air traffic control rather than return to economic regulation. Safety controls have to be strictly enforced and, where necessary, expanded to keep pace with the increase of service which may result from deregulation. In this connection, it is important that the infrastructure of the industry - airport capacity and air control - be improved to cope with increased traffic.

12.   Computer reservation systems have become an important instrument in the marketing of airline tickets. Due to their ownership by the airlines themselves substantial competition issues have arisen relating to the market power through information control which such systems may confer on airlines.

B. CONCLUSIONS AND SUGGESTIONS FOR ACTION

13.   Experience has demonstrated that deregulation and progressive liberalisation produce substantial benefits for efficient air transport services and users. Competition policy approaches based on market-oriented economic strategies constitute a dynamic factor of change as they challenge some of the underlying concepts of economic regulation.

14.   For deregulation to succeed care should be taken that government restrictions should not be replaced by restrictive business practices by airlines. Therefore, it is important that competition laws and policies be enforced in the air transport sector. In some countries transition towards a more competitive market structure will be a gradual one and governments may wish to retain residual authority to intervene in severe instances of market failure. Taking into account the specific characteristics of the industry and a perceived need to smooth the adjustment process, governments may also choose to modulate the enforcement of competition laws in air transport by exemptions targeted to specific practices or situations. In these cases, it is important that such exemptions are granted on a temporary basis and that their justification is regularly reviewed.

15.   Chapter V of this report presents the conclusions and suggestions for action designed to encourage the removal of unnecessary regulatory constraints

and to promote the application of competition laws and policies to passenger air transport. These conclusions and suggestions are summarised below.

a) Entry restrictions, concerted practices, capacity sharing arrangements and rate-fixing

16.   In order for competition to function effectively in the air transport industry, it is essential that entry to the sector and capacity restrictions be liberalised. More liberal market entry allows new or innovative carriers to provide the competitive impetus which can result in increased supply of services and competitive pricing. Without liberalised capacity there may be little space in the market for new competitors or price competition. Governments should therefore review their existing bilateral agreements and seek to eliminate or relax the entry and capacity-restricting provisions in such agreements through renegotiation.

17.   Airlines should have the necessary flexibility to set fares based on their own cost and on market conditions. A great advantage of deregulated fare structures is that it provides consumers with a broader range of choice. Governments should therefore reappraise existing fare approval mechanisms and anti-trust exemptions granted for concerted rate fixing by airlines.

18.   Commercial arrangements between airlines leading to joint or concerted action ("pooling agreements") should be assessed on a rule of reason basis weighing efficiencies created by such agreements against their anticompetitive risks. For this purpose, it is necessary to look separately at each type of agreement to judge whether there is a reasonable balance of benefits between airlines and users and whether there are alternatives to pooling which could serve the same purpose without raising competitive concerns.

19.   Inter-airline agreements to suppress competing services, joint operations between airlines, royalty agreements and capacity and revenue sharing may have strong anti-competitive effects with little redeeming value. Agreements where anti-competitive effects may be off-set by efficiency gains include: co-operation on computer reservation systems, code-sharing and joint scheduling. Under normal circumstances, the following types of agreements would not give rise to competitive concerns: joint undertakings concerning technical and operational ground handling, refuelling and security services, handling of passengers, mail freight and baggage at airports and in-flight catering provided that the sharing of these services is arranged on a non-discriminatory basis and that outside carriers are not excluded from essential facilities at airports.

b) Computer reservation systems

20.   Computer reservation systems are of considerable benefit to users and providers of air transport services in that they can offer a variety of consumer choice and a variety of travel services. At the same time the dominance of CRSs by vendor-carriers has given rise to concern. Because of the technical complexity of CRSs governments should exercise great care so as not to stifle technological progress and innovation in this area. If there are abusive or exclusionary practices by dominant airlines owning computer

reservation systems, competition laws and policies should be applied to remedy such practices.

c) Access to airports and slot allocation

21.   With an increase in air traffic following deregulation as it occurred in the United States access to scarce airport facilities, and in particular gates and slots, has become a crucial issue for competition and this is an area where continued monitoring or regulation may be required to prevent unfair or exclusionary practices by incumbent airlines with market power. Market solutions, e.g. the selling or auctioning of slots, have been proposed, and in one country tried with reasonable success to alleviate problems of access and to avoid recourse by airlines to joint scheduling arrangements. Whether slots are allocated on the basis of market principles or through administrative mechanisms (e.g. by government agencies or airport scheduling committees), government authorities dealing with competition in air transport should take into account these constraints in cases concerning mergers and dominant positions.

d) Mergers, concentration and market power

22.   While concentration in itself is not a sufficient yardstick for measuring the degree of competition, care should be exercised to prevent mergers and acquisitions within concentrated airline markets creating market power and raising the danger of collusion and anti-competitive behaviour.

23.   The following aspects are of particular relevance for the review of mergers in the air transport sector:

-- As a first step the analysis of relevant markets for evaluating the competitive effects of mergers should focus on city pairs;

-- Constraints in essential facilities at busy airports combined with the control of scarce airport slots by merging airlines as well as the dominance of computer reservation systems may constitute significant barriers to entry by new competitors.

24.   Where mergers creating the risk of market power are allowed to proceed in order not to stifle necessary restructuring or efficiency gains, care should be taken that route licences, where they exist, or slots are not automatically transferred through the operation. Rather they should be allocated by the competent authorities or through appropriate divestiture of facilities by the airlines concerned.

25.   Care should be exercised to prevent abuse of market power by dominant carriers through practices such as discriminatory conditions in the use of ground and maintenance facilities under the exclusive control of an airline, biased computer reservation systems and other predatory behaviour.

e) International competition

26.   In accordance with their commitment under the OECD Codes of liberalisation and the National Treatment Instrument, Member countries should consider appropriate action to liberalise trade and investment in air transport services.   To this end, they should review restrictions on investment by non-residents, investment by established foreign-controlled enterprises or any domestic measure of a discriminatory nature.

f) International co-operation in the application of competition laws and policies to passenger air transport

27.   In applying their competition laws and policies to international air transport, Member countries should exercise moderation and restraint and give full and sympathetic consideration to the views expressed by other Member countries whose significant national interests may be affected.   They should continue to co-operate under the 1986 Revised Council Recommendation to avoid or reduce any conflicts which may arise from the concurring application of national competition laws to air transport.

CHAPTER I

CHARACTERISTICS OF THE PASSENGER AIR TRANSPORT SECTOR

1.   Passenger air transport is a major activity in all OECD countries, accounting for a significant share of employment and national income as well as being an important contributor to international trade and to the balance of payments of a number of countries.

2.   The market is segmented into two parts: scheduled and non-scheduled (charter). The industry generally was characterised by very rapid overall growth in the 1950s and 1960s. Traffic by scheduled airlines grew at an average rate of 14 per cent between 1955 and 1969. However in the 1970s, the growth rate fell to 10 per cent (though still high compared with other industries) and the average annual growth dropped to around 3 per cent in the period 1980-3. Asian and Pacific airlines completely changed the structure of the international industry in the 1970s. In 1970, European and North American airlines accounted for three-quarters of international air traffic and by the mid-1980s their share was down to approximately 50 per cent (1).

3.   In the early post-war years, non-scheduled operations were relatively insignificant but they began to grow in the 1960s with the liberalisation of regulations in Europe with respect to charter flights. However, the average annual growth rate from 1975 to 1985 was 8 per cent for international passenger scheduled traffic as a whole but was only 1.7 per cent for non-scheduled traffic, so that the share of non-scheduled passenger traffic has decreased as a proportion of total traffic from 26 per cent in 1975 to 16 percent in 1985 (2).

A. THE EUROPEAN NON-SCHEDULED MARKET

4.   The European charter, or non-scheduled market, has no equivalent elsewhere, not even on the North Atlantic where the share of charter traffic has dropped rapidly in recent years. It is primarily constituted by inclusive tours, i.e. holiday packages, of whose costs the airplane ticket is about a third (3); and aims, naturally, at leisure travellers. Traffic flows are therefore, essentially North-South, serving two main vacation spots in Europe: Spain and Greece. Exceptions to this pattern are the United Kingdom-West Germany route, eighth densest with 800 000 non-scheduled pax, and the United Kingdom-Switzerland (thirteenth, with 550 000 pax). The United Kingdom-Spain route is by far the densest, with ten million pax per year. Spain and the United Kingdom therefore emerge as equally important end points of European charter routes; but the symmetry stops there. Airlines registered in the United Kingdom carry 44 per cent of all intra-European non-scheduled traffic; while airlines registered in Spain carry a mere 8.5 per cent of it. This can

be partly explained by the fact that United Kingdom–Spain traffic is essentially roundtrips departing from and sold in the United Kingdom, so that British airlines are able to capture 85 % of this bilateral traffic. There is however some indication that Spanish airlines are beginning to increase their market share.

5.   It is often claimed that the charter market plays in Europe the same role as the no-frills market does in the deregulated setting of the United States. This may be true in the very broad sense that charter fares are lower than scheduled fares. But it is important to realise that, first, restrictions on the flexibility of charter tickets make them a product very different from no-frills tickets sold in the United States. An important exception to this is the so-called "seat-only" market, on which charter airlines sell airtravel tickets disentangled from holiday packages. Also, the essentially holiday-orientated nature of European charter routes differentiates this traffic from the US.

6.   Table 1 lists the relative importance of scheduled and non-scheduled services in Europe, United States and Japan in 1985. The US domestic market is over twice as large as the European market in terms of passengers and almost three times as large in terms of passenger kilometres. However, even if the existence of significant intermodal competition in Europe is taken into account, there remains a significant difference in output between the two markets, which may indicate a growth potential for European air transport services if regulatory constraints are removed or relaxed. The Japanese scheduled services market amounts to approximately one quarter of the total European market. Another interesting point to emerge from the table is the much larger proportion of non-scheduled traffic in Europe than in the United States. In 1985, non-scheduled traffic, which does not include purely domestic traffic, accounted for 26 per cent of total traffic in Europe by number of passengers and for 42 per cent by passenger/kilometres, whereas in the United States the proportion of non-scheduled is insignificant (less than 1 per cent by both measurements). Non-scheduled domestic traffic in Japan would also appear to be relatively unimportant.

B. NUMBER AND OWNERSHIP OF FIRMS

7.   In Europe, there were in 1985 more than 130 airlines of various kinds (4). The most well-known group consists of twenty-two flag carriers, eighteen of them members of IATA and the AEA (the non-members were Cyprus Airways, GB Air of Gibraltar, Gronlandsfly of Greenland, and Air Malta). This group already shows a high degree of diversity in size, from large airlines such as British Airways, Lufthansa or Air France, to small ones such as Luxair.

8.   There are twenty subsidiaries or associations of national airlines, operating mainly on the non-scheduled market, such as, for instance, Air France's Air Charter, Lufthansa's Condor, or British Airways' British Airtours.

TABLE 1

INTRA-EUROPEAN INTERNATIONAL AND DOMESTIC EUROPEAN
TRAFFIC (1) COMPARED WITH US AND JAPANESE TRAFFIC, 1985

(The figures are preliminary and have been rounded to nearest whole number)

	Passengers carried (millions)	Passenger-kilometres performed (thousand million)
Europe		
Scheduled	120	92
Non-Scheduled (2)	42	67
Total	162	159
United States (3)		
Scheduled	333	418
Non-Scheduled	3	4
Total	336	422
Japan		
Scheduled	45	33

Notes: (1) ECAC Member countries only.
(2) The figures do not take account of purely domestic non-scheduled traffic.
(3) Data relates only to carriers designated by DOT as majors or nationals.

Sources: ICAO Circular 200-AT/78, 1986, Tables 3.8 and Civil Aviation Statistics of the World, ICAO Statistical Year Book 1985, Tables 3.1 and 3.2 for Europe and Table 2.3 for the United States; for Japan, reply to OECD questionnaire.

9.   Twenty-seven other large airlines (i.e. having more than 250 employees) can be found operating mainly on the non-scheduled and regional markets, with some notable exceptions, such as France's Air Inter which has a monopoly over most domestic routes, or Britain's Air U.K., whose charter output represented in 1985 only 1 per cent of its total business. Eight are British, some of them among the largest: Britannia with 4.5 million international non-scheduled passengers, or a market share of 31.4 per cent in the United Kingdom; Air Europe with a market share of 10.4 per cent, Monarch and Orion with less than 10 per cent each (5). The last sixty-one airlines are small - less than 250 employees - being mainly regional, cargo or minor charter passenger airlines.

10.   Public ownership is basically limited to national flag carriers, with in fact numerous exceptions even within this category. Among flag carriers, a first group is made up of ten companies which are more than 80 per cent state-controlled, either directly or through public institutions: Air France, Austrian, Olympic, Aer Lingus, Air Malta, TAP-Air Portugal, Iberia, THY and JAT. Until its recent privatisation, British Airways also belonged to that category.

11.   A second group includes airlines which have between 20 per cent and 50 per cent private participation; this includes Lufthansa (in which Government participation is shared between the Federal Government, Lander and the Deutsche Bundesbahn); Alitalia, whose stockholders are Banca d'Italia, Assicurazioni d'Italia, Banca Nazionale del lavoro, Credito Italiano and IRI; Sabena in which the State has a 54.72 per cent participation; SAS, which is 50 per cent public with 2:2:3 split between Denmark, Norway and Sweden, the three participating states; Finnair, 76 per cent public; and Cyprus Airways.

12.   A third group consists of airlines which are wholly private or have majority private participation: British Airways (since 1986), KLM (39 per cent government participation), Swissair (25 per cent government participation), GB Air (Gibraltar), Luxair, Gronlandsfly, UTA and Icelandair.

13.   In **Australia**, the domestic system of scheduled air passenger services has three broad components: the trunk route airlines which provide major air services on an Australia-wide network using large turbo jet aircraft of 92 to 230 seats; the regional airlines which generally serve more specific geographical areas and use large turbo propeller to small jet aircraft of 44 to 75 seats; and the commuter operators which generally provide air services with small aircraft of 5 to 38 seats on low density short haul routes.

14.   There are only two trunk operators - Ansett and Australian Airlines. Ansett is a private corporation owned by Ansett Transport Industries Limited, and Australian Airlines is a statutory authority of the Government. The decision of the Australian Government, announced in October 1987, to deregulate the domestic aviation industry from 1990 onwards may not result in any dramatic changes to the number of trunk route operators but will enable the development of new operators in response to consumer demand. To enable Australian Airlines to compete effectively in a deregulated environment, the Government is to restructure the airline as a company.

15.   There are five regional airlines, three of which are owned by Ansett and one is owned by Australian Airlines. East-West Airlines is the current major regional airline, and until recently, the only independent. In July 1987, it was acquired by interests associated with Ansett. As the acquisition resulted in these interests dominating some intrastate markets, particularly in Western Australia and New South Wales, agreement was reached with the Trade Practices Commission in November 1987 for the Ansett interests to either divest themselves from or substantially vacate these markets, and to relinquish their controlling interests in a Queensland commuter airline. The effect of this decision also meant that the risk of dominating the interstate or national market was avoided. In the commuter component of the domestic industry, there were 45 operators as of June 1986, although the Government expects this number, and the number of regional operators, to increase in a deregulated environment.

16.   The sole Australian national flag carrier is Qantas. It is a public company wholly owned by the Government, and currently operates scheduled international air services to 30 cities in 23 countries.

17.   In **Canada**, the airline industry has witnessed a dramatic structural reorganisation with the move towards regulatory reform. Two national network systems have emerged: Air Canada, with fully or partially controlled regional and local subsidiaries, Air BC, Austin Airways, Air Ontario, a proposed Quebec feeder line and Air Nova; Canadian Airlines International Ltd. (the amalgamation of Pacific Western Airlines and Canadian Pacific Air Lines), with fully or partially controlled subsidiaries Time Air, Calm Air, Ontario Express, Nordair Metro and Air Atlantic. The above companies also have commercial agreements with other airline companies for feeder traffic, for example, Northwest Territorial Airways and First Air with Air Canada, and Burrard Air and Air St. Pierre with Canadian Airlines International. These two dominant carriers control over 90 per cent of domestic traffic. In addition, the industry is characterized by three major charter airline companies. Wardair Inc. is the country's largest international charter airline and began operating a limited domestic scheduled service in mid 1986. Two other carriers of significant size, Worldways Canada and Nationair Canada, also concentrate on international charter services, although Nationair recently started to operate scheduled flights between Canada and Europe.

18.   While consolidation in the airline industry does offer potential for improvement in efficiency and rivalry between Air Canada and Canadian Airlines International, it also creates a duopoly which potentially can result in a suppression of competition as a result of tacit agreements. The trend towards privatization of the airline industry has continued with the sale of provincial crown corporations, such as Quebecair and Pacific Western Airlines. However, Air Canada remains a federal crown corporation and no decision has been made about future plans to privatize it.

19.   In **Japan**, there are at present seven scheduled air carriers, with four operating on international routes (JAL, AWA, JAA and NCA (cargo only) and five domestic services (JAL, ANA, TDA, SUAL and ANK). JAL accounts for 87 per cent of international services while ANA, TDA and JAL account for 94 per cent of the domestic market, by number of passengers carried. All airlines including JAL are privately owned. In September 1987, the Diet passed a bill to completely privatise JAL; the stock held by the Government was sold in December 1987.

20.   In the **United States**, since deregulation in 1978, the airline industry has both expanded and been consolidated. At the time of deregulation, there were 36 certificated carriers, while today there are 74 certificated carriers. However, the latter figure may understate the degree of concentration: 49 of the carriers operate entirely outside of the 48 contiguous states or have "feeder" agreements with larger carriers, leaving 25 independent competitors in the Continental US. The pace of consolidation has been particularly rapid since late 1985, a period during which there were 23 acquisitions by large carriers.

21.   On an overall nationwide basis the industry has become significantly more concentrated. In January 1986, there were thirteen carriers with annual revenues of over $1 billion; by February 1987 there were only nine airlines in this category. The top four carriers accounted for about 60 per cent of the

total revenue passenger miles. National concentration data, however, do not indicate whether or not airline markets are performing competitively; it is well recognised that competition occurs between carriers providing services between specific city pairs.

C. COSTS AND PERFORMANCE OF THE INDUSTRY

1. Scheduled and charter costs

22.   Some of the direct operating costs of an airline vary directly with the length of a flight; but each flight has some fixed costs: landing fees and ground handling, for instance. It also has quasi-fixed costs: most of the fuel is burnt during take-off, and aircraft wear most when taking off and landing. So even a very short flight involves significant costs.

23.   Similarly, some of the direct operating costs vary, but less than proportionately, with aircraft size: a large aircraft burns more fuel and requires more cabin attendants than a smaller one, but not in proportion to the increase in passengers carried, as large aircraft are both more fuel-efficient and more labour-efficient than smaller ones.

24.   As costs increase less than proportionately with distance and aircraft size, unit costs, i.e. direct operating costs divided by available tonne-kilometres, go down with distance and aircraft size. It is a well-documented fact that deregulation has brought about a rationalisation of the US airlines network, in the form of a shift from a direct-flight system to a hub-and-spoke system, meaning that direct links were, in many cases, replaced by feeder lines (the spokes) converging to a major transit airport (the hub) which was also the end-point of dense, long-haul routes. Thus passengers can be collected from a number of departure points and put together at the "hub" on a flight going to their common destination. This reduces the number of flights and thus allows for greater aircraft size and payload. But, on the other hand, it reduces average stage length on the airlines' networks. The economic consequences of such a change are quite complex. Such a system increases the frequency of possible journeys between end points of spokes, increases the interconnectedness of the network of services, and increases the density of each spoke. On the other hand journey times are likely to increase and some journeys become less convenient as a previous non-stop flight may now involve stops and possible changes of aircraft.

25.   As this change in service pattern was voluntary it is likely that the economies of scale (for aircraft operation) available from increasing route density (i.e. possible move to wide-bodied aircraft), when combined with the advantage to passengers of increased frequency and network connections, outweigh the disadvantages of the increase in costs related to shorter stage lengths and longer total journey lengths, and the decrease in convenience due to longer journey times and changes of plane.

26.   Among direct operating costs, landing fees make a difference as charter airlines generally use cheaper airports. As an illustration, the landing charges at Heathrow at peak periods for most types of aircraft are approximately double the corresponding charges for Gatwick (1987/1988 schedule). Aircraft utilisation is more intensive for charter airlines even though their demand is highly seasonal, due largely to the fact that

short-haul charters fly longer stage lengths than scheduled services. British Airways uses on average its Boeing 757 5.4 hours per day, against 11.7 hours for Air Europe and 9.4 hours for Monarch, both charter lines (6).

27. As load factors are much higher (85 per cent on average against 65 per cent for scheduled airlines) and seating configurations are 15 to 25 per cent denser in chartered aircraft, non-scheduled airlines get 50 to 63 per cent more passengers in each aircraft, and realize, under this single heading, cost savings of 33 to 39 per cent. It should be noted, however, that high load factors reflect a lower degree of flexibility in booking and therefore diminish the quality of the service offered. As for seating density, the effect on travel pleasure is obvious.

28. Other important cost savings are realised in indirect operating costs. While scheduled airlines principally sell a retail product, charters sell wholesale and thus the bulk of marketing costs are incurred by tour operators. Subcontracting for passenger, luggage and aircraft ground handling at destination airports and seasonal employment contribute to the savings. But the most is realised from the absence of computer reservation systems, of advertising, and of agents' commissions, as charter airlines generally sell to a small number of large tour operators. In the United Kingdom, for instance, less than fifty tour operators charter ninety per cent of the flights. Therefore marketing costs per pax are extremely low, ranging in 1982 from almost nothing for Orion to £0.08 for Britannia against £22.37 for British Caledonian and £18.15 for British Airways.

2. Profitability

29. Despite the unusually high rate of growth in the industry throughout most of the last 30 years as well as the existence of falling unit costs, the profitability of the airline industry as a whole has been marginal. Doganis (7) distinguishes five distinct phases: (i) up to 1960, profit margins were low and in a number of years there were net losses. This is attributed to high unit operating costs; (ii) in the 1960s, unit costs declined, producing a dramatic improvement in profit margins, despite a fall in load factors and falling fares; (iii) by 1968, load factors had fallen to less than 50 per cent and continued to decline. This, together with rising unit costs, affected profit margins. The airlines made determined efforts to improve load factors after the oil price crisis of 1973-1974 increased fuel prices by 300 per cent in a few months. Added to widespread inflation and the downturn in economic growth plus a fall in demand for both passenger and freight transport, this price increase led to a large increase in unit costs in 1974-1975; (iv) from 1975-8, there was a profitable period due to a fall in the price of fuel and other costs in real terms and due to the fact that demand was buoyant; (v) however from 1979, the airlines entered a period of crisis provoked by a further dramatic increase in fuel prices and stagnating demand due to the world-wide recession.

30. After paying interest, IATA member airlines (together with Pan Am) collectively lost $350 million on their international scheduled services in 1979. In 1980 the net loss was $1 850 million; the following year it was $1 900 million, and in 1982 it was marginally lower, at $1 800 million. The loss was about $300 million in 1983 but in 1984 a profit of $800 million was realised. In 1985, the profit was $200 million followed by a loss of

$200 million in 1986. For 1987 a profit of $600 million is estimated (8). Much of each year's loss was due to high interest payments on loans for aircraft or for bank overdrafts. IATA members' overall financial results including domestic and charter services were somewhat better than the above figures, which refer solely to international scheduled services.

31.   As Doganis points out, the continuing marginal profitability of the industry is the major problem facing the airlines during the 1980s. However, it should be borne in mind that overall figures do not preclude the profitability of individual carriers or groups of carriers. In the United States, it would seem that the main beneficiaries of deregulation have been the regional carriers and those trunk carriers who have adapted most quickly to deregulation (see Annex II, p. 113).

3. Factors influencing the demand for passenger air services

32.   The demand for passenger air services is a derived demand dependent on the passenger's demand for other activities such as business trips, holidays or other leisure-time pursuits. The market is therefore segmented into two main parts due to the fact that in the case of business travel the passenger is usually not paying for his own trip but is in the case of leisure travel. In all OECD countries it would seem that the overall proportion of business travel -- when both scheduled and non-scheduled traffic is considered -- is below 30 per cent and for the United Kingdom it is below 20 per cent. However on certain scheduled routes business travel may account for the bulk of total traffic. In the United Kingdom in 1983 almost half of the United Kingdom residents flying abroad went on inclusive tours, the majority on charter flights.

33.   The motivation for travel has an impact both on frequency of travel and on the duration, business travellers tending to fly more frequently and taking shorter trips. Conversely, leisure travellers tend to take longer trips and less frequently.

34.   The second characteristic of demand is the marked peaks and troughs in demand (daily, weekly and seasonal). Peak flows require extra capacity which may be under-utilized during off-peak periods. Seasonal peaks result mainly from holiday patterns and religious festivals. They are particularly relevant to non-scheduled operators and pose particular problems. Non-scheduled carriers attempt to overcome this problem by intensive use of aircraft during the peak season and may lease aircraft to other parts of the world with a different seasonal pattern.

35.   Scheduled service airlines may be able to meet peak demands by shifting aircraft of different sizes between routes. However, they are constrained from doing this by the simultaneous appearance of peaks in many markets and by the inability of regulatory structure to allow such shifts. The inter-government or inter-airline agreement under which a specific route is flown may be aircraft-size specific. Altering the aircraft size may, therefore, involve getting permission from the aeronautical authorities and/or the other airlines involved. Aeronautical authorities may also place a premium on regularity of service which constrains airlines from meeting peak demand by altering service frequencies.

36.   In addition, airlines are constrained by the price regulations from trying to smooth out the daily peaks by peak pricing. To a certain extent they can limit the availability of some "discount" tickets to flights with relatively low demand but except for a few exceptions explicit off-peak and peak pricing is not allowed in most international markets. However, limited seasonal pricing especially for discount tickets is often possible so that in those markets with significant seasonal variations of demand explicit pricing policies that help to smooth the demand pattern are available.

37.   Of the general factors affecting demand for air services, the price of air transport and the level of personal income appear to be the two most important. Most of the growth in air transport in the last 30 years can be attributed to falling real fares and rising incomes. Most studies have concluded, as might be expected, that demand for leisure travel is sensitive to price and income changes, whereas demand for business travel is less elastic. This fact has led airlines to differentiate their fares according to customer and explains the diversity of fares currently available on scheduled flights.

38.   In summary, the structure and operation of the air transport industry is in the process of change which will be accelerated by deregulation measures taken in various countries. In an internationalised economy, there are strong pressures towards increased efficiency and the trend away from rigid regulatory structures could well be irreversible. Deregulation has been carried furthest in the United States, where since the early 1980s carriers have been free to enter any domestic route and to charge whatever fares they choose. While not so extensive as in the United States, other countries, too, have begun to adopt more liberal licensing policies. For example, in Canada, Southern Canadian air services have been considerably liberalised since 1985. In the United Kingdom, domestic passenger air services have undergone partial liberalisation. Recently considerable interest has centred on the proposals for liberalising the European market put forward by the Commission of the European Communities and recently adopted by the Council of Ministers.

D. COMPETITIVE STRUCTURE OF THE AIRLINE INDUSTRY

39.   There is no consensus among airline economists about the exact nature of the industry. Those in favour of regulation have traditionally argued that the industry is either a natural monopoly or an interdependent oligopoly requiring regulation to ensure that fares are not raised above competitive levels. Another view is that the industry is prone to excessive entry by airlines with little prospect of success or by "cream-skimmers" which will serve only the more attractive routes and which will undermine the integrated network which can be achieved by internal cross-subsidy in a regulated market. Others view the industry as structurally competitive due to the threat of entry which is considered effective in keeping prices down to their competitive level - variations on the contestability theory. Empirical evidence is not convincing for any theory. A crucial assumption of the contestability theory is that the market in question has no sunk costs such as advertising and irrecoverable capital investment, making "hit and run" entry or the threat of it possible. It has however been found that the assumption of no sunk costs does not hold in the airline industry. In actual empirical testing a number of barriers to entry have been found to exist, notably the limited availability of airport slots and gates as well as the existence of

computer reservation systems (9). Barnes (10) in his paper on the impact of partial liberalisation of UK domestic air transport found that the main impetus to lower fares came from the actual entry of a new competitor on a particular route and not from the simple threat of entry as contestability theory implies. The overwhelming consensus in United States literature is that airline markets are not perfectly contestable and that they should therefore be treated like any other market: not regulated but subject to the antitrust laws.

40.   Some evidence on the existence of economies of scale and scope does exist. Larger aircraft are generally more efficient than smaller ones. However, these economies do not appear very significant. A recent Canadian study (11) found significant economies of stage length and economies of density, i.e. economies achieved when output growth is within a network of fixed size, and mild economies of scale, i.e. when output growth is due to increasing network size. Several studies have attempted to test for the influence of various measures of market concentration, including the number of firms, on observed fares. Graham, Kaplan and Sibley (12), have found that concentration, measured by the Herfindahl index, does influence fares, but by less than might be expected from traditional, i.e. pre-contestability, theory. Call and Keeler (13) have, however, criticized their entry variable, arguing that they should have considered only entry by established and reputed airlines; entry by newly certificated carriers constitutes, according to them, little threat to powerful incumbents. Their own study showed a significant effect of market concentration on fares. Morrison and Winston found that potential entry matters only when there is a relatively large number of prospective entrants (14). Two recent studies by US Department of Justice economists have also found that concentration does have an effect on airline yields (15).

41.   Another recent study (16) has shown that cost savings reaped through network rationalisation, such as replacement of a direct flight network by hub-and-spoke entails significant economies of scope: entrants are free to come in but cannot offer lower fares on direct flights than the incumbent offers through its hub-and-spoke system nor can they effectively compete in a part of this system because they would not reap full cost savings. On the other hand the incumbent may not be able to charge supra-competitive prices because at that point it would become vulnerable to competition from direct flights.

42.   The tentative conclusion that can be drawn from these studies as well as the experience with deregulation is that the air transport sector has some economies of scale and scope so that there will never be room for numerous airlines competing on each route but that even with some sunk costs, new entry can be a significant competitive force so that an incumbent airline is not generally able to reap monopoly profits for a non-transitory period unless regulation distorts the market.

E. INTERMODAL COMPETITION

43.   Since air transport, as a service, may have close substitutes in the form of rail and road transport, it is interesting to see how well the air transport industry competes with these other modes. Each air route being, in fact, a separate market, the conditions of competition vary greatly from route

to route, according, in particular, to distance. An interesting comparison of the modal split in the United States and in Europe in the 1970s (17) shows that the main difference is the importance, in Europe, of traffic taken up by rail in the range between 400 and 1 500 km, basically at the expense of air transport. The second difference is the decrease in the importance of car transportation over long distances in Europe, while it still represents a third of all traffic in the 2 000 km range in the United States. The European air transport market is therefore weak in the 1 000 km range (less than 25 per cent of all traffic) and strong in the 2 000 km range (more than 75 per cent of traffic) while its United States counterpart is more evenly spread (30 per cent in the 1 000 km range, 55 per cent in the 2 000). Since the average European flight length is about 1 000 km, competition by rail appears as an important competitive factor on the European air transport market.

44.   While doubling aircraft speed from 500 to 1 000 km/h merely reduces total travel time by 15 per cent, doubling train speed from 130 to 260 km/h - i.e. switching from regular train to TGV - reduces total travel time by a third. The effect on the competitive range of rail is even more dramatic as compared to air transport: a TGV is faster, on a door-to-door basis, from 0 to more than 500 km, against 0 to slightly less than 200 km in the case of an ordinary train. The introduction of TGV can therefore be expected to have a strong impact on the competitiveness of air transportation.

45.   This is confirmed by the evolution of traffic on several routes from Paris to Southern France. The effect of the introduction of the TGV is dramatically apparent, as the Paris-Lyon route lost half of its traffic between 1980 and 1985, while other routes saw their own traffic grow by 50 to 150 per cent; routes served by the TGV, but less efficiently than Paris-Lyon stagnated throughout the period, in contrast with non TGV routes.

F. OTHER FACTORS AFFECTING COMPETITION

46.   There are two particular constraints on entry and on effective competition among airlines - the restriction on access to particular airports due to the limited availability of airport slots and gates and the increasing use of computer reservation systems operated by the dominant airline and which may discriminate against smaller airlines or be a deterrent to new entry.

1. Airport access

47.   An air transport route has to involve the use of at least two airports and, in most cases, an individual air transport market involves the use of two specific airports. Access to these airports is, therefore, a necessary condition for an airline to have access to a particular market. If airport access is constrained there cannot be free access to the markets served by that airport, even if no other constraints are placed on an airline wanting to serve those markets (i.e. if there is free route entry). The real competition concern is that a carrier possessing all or a large percentage of slots at a capacity-constrained airport may have market power.

48.   Practices in member countries vary with respect to slot allocation. In Europe, in the absence of specific regulations, the allocation of slots is governed by agreements between airlines following guidelines issued by the

International Air Transport Association (IATA). This results in a system where airlines having a slot in the previous period can retain it indefinitely as long as they continue operating. Unused slots or slots which have become vacant are allocated among airlines following a hierarchy of uses set out in the IATA Guidelines. Final decisions are made by airport scheduling committees which are usually composed of existing airlines using the airport. Individual airlines can use their slots without any major restriction changing routes, for example, or swapping slots with other airlines.

49.   In the United States, take-off and landing at four important airports are subject to federal regulations. Incumbent airlines using these airports were given "grandfather rights"; unused slots or those falling vacant are reallocated by the Federal Aviation Administration (FAA) and airlines are free to buy and sell slots at market prices.

50.   Because timing is of critical importance in the scheduled air transport markets, an airport that is working at full capacity for any length of time can effectively exclude new entrant airlines from most of the routes using that airport, and thus from most of the markets served by that airport. In addition, because slots are airline specific an airline with a significant proportion of the slots will have considerably more timetabling flexibility in any one market served by that airport than an airline with a limited number of slots. This condition holds even if the first airline does not dominate any particular market. At most airports the slot allocation mechanism and other necessary co-ordination between the airlines and the airport is administered by the dominant airline although not in the United States where slots can be bought and sold in the open market. Landing and other charges are set unilaterally by the airport owner and/or their governments, but these charges may be subject to a "reasonableness" clause in the bilateral agreement(s) and by a similar declaration made by the government to ICAO. (However, whether these "reasonableness" clauses could be enforced remains open to question.)

2. Airline Computer reservation systems (CRSs)

51.   In recent years, several airlines have developed CRSs in response to the increased demand for air services due largely to deregulation and liberalisation. Originally developed to automate passenger seat reservation and ticketing processes, new technology has increased the capacity and functions of the systems, so that the majority of seats are now sold by means of these systems, especially in the United States where 95 per cent of all US travel agents are equipped with one or more CRSs, which account for 70 per cent of all ticket sales.

52.   Several United States carriers, notably United and American, have invested heavily in the development of their CRSs - Apollo and Sabre - which as of May 1987 controlled 68 per cent of the terminals installed at travel agents. European CRSs have not traditionally been highly competitive - tending to operate within the borders of their home countries and offering a more limited range of services.

53.   There are two main interrelated competition issues raised by CRSs - CRSs bias and market domination. Until 1984, the screens of US vendor-carriers were biased in favour of their own flights. CRS bias involved a competitor's flights appearing on a later computer screen than the flights

of the vendor-carrier even when they were more direct or convenient or less expensive. In 1984 the US Civil Aeronautics Board issued regulations to require that CRS primary displays not be based on any factor "directly or indirectly related to carrier identity" but on the basis of consistently applied service criteria. However the issue has not been totally resolved as several antitrust cases have been filed on this issue (see Annex I, paragraph 17).

54.   The problem of CRS bias has also arisen internationally. Under the US International Air Transportation Fair Competition Practices Act, three US carriers - Northwest Airlines, TWA and Pan American - filed a complaint against Lufthansa, and the Federal German Government to have approval of the pending Frankfurt - Houston Lufthansa service held up until the bias against US carriers was eliminated from the Lufthansa system START. Also, in 1986, the UK expressed concern that the criteria for display still contained significant biases against international operators, substantially limiting their access to the US market.

55.   As regards the market domination issue, the main concern is whether individual CRS suppliers will be able to dominate the main method of marketing the industry's product. The subsidiary issues are whether access charges for participating carriers are reasonable as well as whether liquidated damage clauses in contracts with travel agencies act as a barrier to entry and whether the functions of yield management, and access to competitors' information brought about by CRS are anticompetitive in that they allow carriers to develop strategies to counteract their rivals' tariff policies. The high capital and operating costs as well as long-term supply contracts also may constitute a formidable barrier to entry on the part of smaller or medium-sized carriers. Indeed, it is the smaller carriers which have often expressed concern about CRS bias and dominance issues. In the United States, concern over the information access issue has led to the adoption of CRS rules requiring vendors to sell marketing data to all carriers on a non-discriminatory basis.

CHAPTER II

THE REGULATORY FRAMEWORK

A. THE INTERNATIONAL FRAMEWORK OF AIR TRANSPORT REGULATION

1. Intergovernmental co-operation

56.   There is limited competition between airlines in international air travel due to the existence of bilateral government agreements regulating routes, capacity and tariffs. Some segments of the industry do however operate under conditions of price competition, for example the non-scheduled sector in Europe, where individual operators are not obliged to co-operate on tariffs and routes with other non-scheduled airlines.

57.   The basic instrument governing international civil aviation is the Chicago Convention of 1944 which regulates both scheduled and non-scheduled international air services. The Convention successfully established multilateral agreement in some areas but not in relation to commercial rights which were left to bilateral agreements to be negotiated between countries. The Convention also established the International Civil Aviation Organisation (ICAO) as a permanent international forum to oversee safety standards.

58.   The Chicago Convention is adhered to by the 157 Member States of ICAO. It is based on the principle that "every state has complete and exclusive sovereignty over the airspace above its territory". Thus international air services require the permission of governments to operate. The Convention therefore established that scheduled air services between countries would be subject to bilateral agreement. Non-scheduled services would be treated differently "without the necessity of obtaining prior permission". In practice, however, each individual state is free to impose whatever conditions or restrictions it considers desirable on non-scheduled services so that although not generally covered by the bilateral regime, non-scheduled services do in fact require permission and are subject to regulation, though more liberal policies are pursued by most States in regard to non-scheduled services.

59.   The Chicago Convention also established the rights to be granted to airlines flying scheduled services as five different "freedoms":

    i) to overfly a country without stopping;

    ii) to land and take off for technical purposes (ie. to refuel, change crew, etc.);

26

iii) to take passengers and cargo from the home country to the foreign country;

iv) to take passengers and cargo from the foreign country to the home country;

v) to take passengers and cargo from the foreign country to a third country or vice-versa.

60.   As already mentioned, however, the Convention failed to agree on multilateral rules for the five freedoms but did agree to all the freedoms being granted in bilateral agreements (1). A multilateral agreement covering the first two freedoms was subsequently drawn up outside the Conference and adopted – the International Transit Agreement to which most of the signatories to the Chicago Convention also acceded.

61.   There is at present an extensive network of bilateral agreements (2). The 1946 agreement between the United Kingdom and the United States (Bermuda 1) was the model for many of these bilateral arrangements. These agreements generally take the following form although there is wide variation:

a) scheduled air services between two countries provided by one or more airlines designated by each country to provide the services;

b) an airline designated by a country must be substantially owned and effectively controlled by the country designating it or by nationals of that country;

c) the tariffs for tickets should be agreed between the airlines, approved by the airlines' international association, IATA, and approved by both governments;

d) the capacity provided by each airline on each route should not unduly affect the services provided by the other airline;

e) each country's airlines should have fair and equal opportunity to operate on the routes between the countries;

f) the routes (city to city) to be operated are specified in the agreement (or in schedules attached to the agreement);

g) on some routes it may be possible to take passengers from the home country to the foreign country and fly some of them on to another airport in that country or a third country (and vice versa);

h) on some routes it may be possible to pick up passengers in the other country and take them to a third country (and vice versa).

62.   In three of the Nordic countries – Denmark, Norway and Sweden – aviation policy is coordinated by an agreement concluded in 1951 when the Scandinavian Airline System (SAS) was instituted.

63.   In recent years, the United Kingdom and the United States in particular have been renegotiating their air service agreements with some Members of the European Civil Aviation Conference (ECAC) (3), notably with Belgium, the

Netherlands, Germany, Luxembourg, France and Switzerland, with the aim of liberalising the bilateral arrangements. In general terms, the air service agreements are very restrictive so that capacity, prices and routes have to be set with the agreement of the aeronautical authorities at both ends of the route. For example, the United Kingdom/Finland agreement allows only one route to be served, London to Helsinki, and does not allow any other destination to be combined with this. However, not all agreements are restrictive. A number of them have never significantly restricted routes (e.g. the former United Kingdom/Netherlands agreement). In addition to the actual agreements, confidential memoranda of understanding are frequently agreed to restrict and regulate air services even further, including capacity as well as routes, frequently combined with revenue pooling arrangements to ensure more or less equal revenue to the airlines operating a particular route. Other arrangements however provide for the allocation of revenue in proportion to capacity (e.g. the former United Kingdom/Germany air service agreement). Thus, the freedom in some air service agreements to pick up passengers in a foreign country and fly to a third country (the fifth freedom) is rare in Europe, and where it does exist this freedom is usually very tightly capacity controlled.

64.   The bilateral agreements usually consist of three parts – the agreement itself, an annex and a memorandum of understanding. In the agreement itself the two key articles relate to the regulation of tariffs and capacity providing for approval of both by both governments. The annex contains the schedule of routes where the traffic rights reciprocally granted are made explicit. The schedule specifies the routes to be operated by the designated airline(s) of each State as well as the points to be served. Each State is free to designate its own airline(s) subsequently for these routes. The schedule also indicates whether any fifth freedom rights are granted, i.e. whether the designated airlines are free to pick up passengers in other countries or points between the two States. This is of course subject to the agreement of any third countries involved. The final part of the bilateral is often confidential and modifies particular aspects of the basic agreement. Foreign carriers are generally excluded from competition on domestic routes (cabotage). In addition, foreign investment or investment by foreign controlled enterprises in the air transport sector is restricted in many Member countries.

65.   Perhaps the greatest prospect for increased competition in the scheduled air services market lies in more liberal bilateral agreements. The Netherlands/United Kingdom agreement as modified in 1984 and 1985 is a good example of the possibility of reducing the regulation. It provides for freer access to routes, no restrictions on capacity, no prior consultation between the airlines on tariffs to be filed and allowance of tariffs unless disapproved by both aeronautical authorities. Also the bilateral agreement between Australia and the United States provides that neither party to the agreement can block fares which have been approved for travel commencing in the territory of the other parts.

66.   In the last two years a number of developments have indicated a trend towards globalisation of the industry and a more multilateral approach to air transport negotiations. The Dutch carrier KLM has taken a 14.9 per cent share in the British carrier Air UK. The Irish carrier Ryan Air has purchased the UK carrier London European and SAS made an unsuccessful bid for the UK carrier British Caledonian.

67.   The tendency for cross-frontier mergers has been encouraged by several
factors: privatisation   of   largely   state-owned   carriers;   perceived
competitive pressure from large US carriers and the development of joint
computer reservation systems.   This trend is likely to accelerate as
cross-frontier mergers tend to weaken the national identity of carriers air
transport negotiation could become increasingly multilateral in scope.

68.   On the basis of its policy an intra-European air transport declaration,
adopted at its 12th triannual session the European Civil Aviation Conference
(ECAC) which, in addition to the EC Member countries, includes 10 other
Western European countries, is undertaking efforts towards liberalisation of
air transport throughout Western Europe.   As the result of a diplomatic
conference ECAC has adopted on 16th June 1987 multilateral agreements on
tariffs (signed by 14 countries) and capacity sharing (signed by 10
countries).   The agreements expand the possibilities of discounts without
prior government authorisation and abandon the traditional principle of 50 per
cent capacity sharing among carriers of different countries.   Parallel to the
efforts of the EC, work is undertaken on market access, interregional services
and computer reservation systems.

69.   As already noted the bilateral air service agreements do not in general
cover non-scheduled services which fall in principle under a different section
of the Chicago Convention which lays down a multilateral régime.   In practice,
however, non-scheduled flights are also frequently subject to regulation by
national governments, although more liberal licensing policies are sometimes
pursued and the conditions are less stringently enforced than in the case of
scheduled services.   In 1956, the Member States of the ECAC agreed to waive
the requirement for prior authorisation from the destination country for a
wide range of non-scheduled flights.   Thus, non-scheduled services have tended
to be relatively free from international regulation, while still being subject
to national rules on licensing and tariffs (see next section).   However, the
following conditions are sometimes required for non-scheduled flights:

   a) the operator of the aircraft must not sell tickets either
      individually or direct to the public;

   b) the tickets for the flight must be part of an overall package that
      includes accommodation (or other ground facility);

   c) minimum and/or maximum length of stay;

   d) freight is not carried with passengers on the same aircraft;

   e) the service will not adversely affect the interests of the scheduled
      airlines and their regular services.

70.   In addition, the airline operator may have to submit a complete
description of the flight, the aircraft to be used, the tour operators
chartering the aircraft and of the "ground packages" to be used.   Some
countries also impose price controls on the cost of the package usually
related to prices charged on an equivalent scheduled route.

71.   The main feature of the regulation of non-scheduled services is that
airlines negotiate only with the governments concerned for permission to fly

and, unlike scheduled operations, there is no regulatory requirement to co-operate with other operators on that route.

2. Self-regulation through IATA

72.   While the bilateral agreements do not provide for control of fares, these have been in many cases regulated through IATA. The International Air Transport Association (IATA) which was set up in 1944 is a trade association composed of most international scheduled airlines and provides the machinery for regulating tariffs and routes by agreement, subject to the quasi automatic approval by governments. However, agreement is sometimes not reached within IATA and individual governments frequently refuse to approve fare increases agreed in IATA. By resolution O45, IATA had obliged its members to refrain from certain "charter" operations, although IATA rules permit its scheduled airline members to undertake non-scheduled operations subject to certain conditions. In 1946, IATA imposed the maximum limitation on non-scheduled operations so as to protect the scheduled services and this system remained in force for many years, with the effect that no charter company could sell at below IATA fares. IATA has now instituted policies permitting airlines to participate in its trade association activities without joining the fare setting process.

73.   The development of inclusive tour charters (ITCs) by non-scheduled operators was encouraged by the European Civil Aviation Conference, involving the purchase of a flight and ground package at an all-inclusive price, thus differentiating the product from the "travel only" service. In order to compete in this market, many IATA members established non-IATA charter subsidiaries and/or started to sell blocks of their capacity on scheduled services to tour operators at prices significantly below the prices for individual tickets. Thus there arose both scheduled and non-scheduled services being operated by the same airlines and lower priced restricted fares on scheduled services, which injected more competition into certain routes, especially on routes such as the North Atlantic, where both types of operation exist in parallel. The advent of low-price non-fully flexible fares and of low cost/low price airlines in the North Atlantic market has had a very significant effect on fares there.

B. DESCRIPTION OF EXISTING NATIONAL REGULATIONS

74.   In addition to the bilateral and multilateral arrangements, air transport is also subject to extensive national regulation in almost all OECD countries. Much of this regulation is of the non-economic type, concerned with technical and safety standards based on ICAO standards and practices. While these regulations undoubtedly constrain airline operation, they are applied to all airlines and therefore do not distort competition between individual airlines.

75.   However in most countries there are also comprehensive economic regulations. In the first place operations require licences issued by the appropriate authority (aviation authority or transport ministry) which are based on varying economic criteria which do affect competitive conditions. Generally speaking, more stringent economic criteria apply to applicants wishing to operate scheduled services, being based on some showing of a public

need for the additional service. In addition, the licence usually specifies the conditions of operation, covering the domestic routes to be operated, capacity and fares, with fare changes being subject to prior approval by the authorities. However, in the United Kingdom, it is not usual to limit capacity or frequency except where there are limited available traffic rights. The notable exception to this regulatory scenario is the United States where since the early 1980s a certificate to engage in air transport is awarded to any US person who is fit, willing and able to do so and no restriction is placed on the rates, fares or capacity of persons holding such certificates.

76.   Otherwise the aviation authorities exercise control over most aspects of civil aviation activity subject in some cases to appeal. As regards licences for scheduled services, the licensed airline can operate only on routes specifically designated in the authorisation and the Authority has a variety of sanctions available to it in the event that the airline infringes the terms and condition of its licence ranging from revocation, alteration or suspension. Australia has a unique system in that air traffic on the major national or trunk routes is largely reserved for two airlines as a result of a long-standing agreement between the two airlines in question since 1952. The agreement in turn is supported by a complex package of measures which allows the Government to control aircraft capacity, entry onto trunk routes and fare pricing. However, this system of control will come to an end in 1990 when the present agreement expires. The Australian Government announced in October 1987 that it would withdraw from detailed economic regulation of domestic aviation but, as the terms of the airlines agreement require three years notice of termination, it is not possible to accomplish this deregulation before 1990.

77.   The regulation of non-scheduled services is much less stringent in some countries. For example in the United Kingdom, it is normal to grant licences for inclusive tour charters without specifying the routes and it is not usual to limit capacity or frequency. In addition, fares for non-scheduled flights are not subject to regulation. In the United Kingdom, the procedure for granting licences for scheduled services is usually open, that is to say a public hearing is held by the licensing authority where holders of existing licences may voice objections to applications for new licences or to variations in existing ones or wide ranging consultations are held with all interested parties, taking account of public demand.

78.   As regards subsidies or other forms of government assistance to airlines, a few countries reported the existence of some assistance for essential services not financially viable. For example, in Canada, the National Transportation Act (NTA) provides for the possibility of subsidies for air transport to remote locations when loss of commercial service occurs. Subsidized service is provided by the most economic carrier after an open competition is held to provide the service. In Australia, in recent years, a capital injection of $115 million was given to Australian Airlines, on statutory authority of the Government, to help it compete more effectively with Ansett. As regards the Nordic countries, until 1st October 1987 there was a formal State guarantee against SAS losses subject to repayment. This guarantee no longer exists but was applied once, in 1961. In Norway, the firm Widerboe which operates on domestic regional scheduled routes receives subsidies from the Government. In addition, it should be noted that there is an extensive amount of cross-subsidisation between domestic routes in Norway

for reasons of regional policy. In Finland, certain local services are subsidised by the municipalities concerned. In Portugal certain subsidies are given by the Government and in Spain the government compensates the airlines which are legally bound to grant discounts on reference fares between the mainland and the Canary and Balearic Islands for the inhabitants of these islands. In the United Kingdom, prior to April 1984, British Airways' outstanding borrowings and finance leases were government guaranteed and part of the airline's debt benefited from government exchange rate risk cover.

79.   Until the end of 1987, in the European Communities, the rules applicable to air transport included a 1979 Decision relating to a consultation procedure on relations between Member States and third countries in the field of air transport, a 1980 Directive on accident investigation (4) and a 1983 Directive on interregional air services (5). The last Directive goes in the direction of liberalisation of scheduled air services. Tariff approval has been made much easier in that it does not involve other airlines or IATA and the determination of fares is related to the costs of the air carrier. This Directive, however, involves only a very specific segment of the market: in particular, aircraft must have less than seventy seats and not use a major airport at either end of the route. Therefore, while very substantial for the services covered, the results of the implementation of this Directive remain of limited scope and relatively few new services have been developed. As noted in the report from the Commission to the Council on the operation of that Directive "since the Directive was approved by the Council in 1983, a number of new bilateral agreements have been concluded in the Community which, inter alia, provide for greater freedom of market access than the provisions established by the Directive". Consequently, the European Commission proposed amendments to the existing Directive a number of which were adopted. The Directive now allows new services between a smaller airport and a "category one" airport, often the largest airport in each country.

80.   Following intensive negotiations the Council adopted on 14th December 1987 a package of measures to increase competition in the civil aviation sector. These measures, which took effect on 1st January 1988, comprise (i) Council Regulation (EEC) No. 3975/87 of 14th December 1987 laying down the procedure for the application of the rules of competition to the air transport sector; (ii) Council Regulation (EEC) No. 3976/87 of 14th December 1987 on the application of Article 85(3) of the Treaty to certain categories of agreements and concerted practices in the air transport sector; (iii) Council Directive of 14th December 1987 on fares for scheduled air services between Member States; and (iv) Council Decision of 14th December 1987 on the sharing of passenger capacity between air carriers on scheduled air services between Member States and on access for air carriers to scheduled air service routes between Member States (6).

81.   The package is a first step towards the completion of the internal market in air transport. While Member States will remain competent for their bilateral relations in air transport, the scope for the exercise of their sovereignty has been substantially reduced by the various measures, in particular since the system whereby both governments must agree on fares, capacity and airline designation has now been changed and objective criteria must be respected. Thus, for capacity a Member State will only be able to act to maintain its airlines' capacity share if that share falls below 45 per cent (or, after 1.10.1989, 40 per cent) of the total capacity mounted on all services between two Member States. There is thus scope for additional

competition between airlines. This scope is reinforced by the greater possibilities afforded to airlines to set their own fares and, in particular, to relate their fares to their own costs rather than to the fares of other carriers. Moreover, there is provision for automatic approval of certain discount and deep discount fares. The fares directive lays down criteria which Member States must respect in approving fares and provides for arbitation, whose results are binding on governments, in the event of a disagreement. Finally, possibilities are opened up for new carriers to come on to particular routes, both in the context of multiple designation on the main Community routes and of fifth freedom operations. New traffic rights are created between the major airports and the regional airports, and this creates new possibilities for competition between hubs on connecting services. These access provisions are particularly significant, as empirical evidence suggests that it is the presence of a new competitor on a route (rather than the threat of his arrival) which makes the difference to the level of fares.

C. POOLING AGREEMENTS

82.   Capacity agreements and pooling arrangements are usually linked. As the previous sections in this chapter have shown, capacity agreements are an essential feature of bilateral agreements, while inter-airline pooling arrangements may form part of the airline commercial agreements which translate the bilateral government decisions on capacity and other issues into daily practice. In addition, airlines have tended to supplement the formal agreements with confidential understandings and side agreements which may substantially modify the practice provided for in the published agreements. However, in some cases, inter-airline agreements have not been concluded to give effect to the bilateral capacity sharing arrangements.

83.   The term "pooling" is often loosely applied to take in all the elements of airline commercial agreements. In its narrower sense, it involves only the totality of revenue assigned from earnings on one or more routes by the pool partners for the purpose of determining the size of the overall "cake" to be divided between them under a revenue sharing arrangement. For the purposes of this report, pooling will be considered in its broader sense as the principal aspects of commercial agreements which lead to joint or concerted action by airlines, whether or not they involve the sharing of revenues.

84.   Capacity sharing has a direct influence on several other aspects of airline agreements. Capacity restrictions strongly affect market entry, since if capacity sharing is not eased, there may be little space in the market for new competitors. It also has an influence on tariffs: if capacity is restricted, there is less opportunity for new entrants or existing carriers on the routes to offer experimental or discount fares.

85.   According to the European Civil Aviation Conference's COMPAS Report, some 93 per cent of intra-ECAC bilateral agreements had capacity provisions of some kind in 1982, the year the Report was written (7). This figure would have to be revised downward somewhat because of intervening events, notably some of the liberal bilaterals that have been negotiated between the UK and several European countries, though even some of these, such as the UK-France agreement, have retained fairly rigid capacity controls. According to the COMPAS Report, 30 per cent of the European capacity agreements were regulated

33

by frequency of flights, around 10 per cent by proportions or numbers of seats or passengers.

86.   The COMPAS Report also noted that between 75 and 85 per cent of the tonne-kilometres performed on intra-European scheduled flights were performed under pooling agreements. None of the pooling agreements involve more than two airlines and with few exceptions they only involve intra-European routes.

87.   According to the COMPAS Report, European pools are characterized by the following features:

    i)   Virtually all cover scheduled services only;

   ii) Approximately 80 per cent cover passengers and cargo; 15 per cent cover passengers only;

  iii) All involve revenue sharing, 80 per cent with limitations, 20 per cent without;

   iv) Between 10 and 15 per cent involve cost sharing;

    v) Between 15 and 20 per cent limit the capacity which can be provided by one of the pool partners and a larger proportion limit the total capacity provided by the pool;

   vi) Approximately two-thirds involve agreement on frequencies to be operated;

  vii) Approximately one-third involve forward planning for periods of more than 12 months ahead of capacity, load factors, and frequency (8).

Since the survey was taken, it is likely that more carriers have tended to concentrate on the capacity planning and coordination features of pooling and some reportedly have decided that pooling has outlived its usefulness. For example, British Airways has withdrawn from most and is withdrawing from the rest of its pooling agreements in Europe.

88.   Although the ceiling (often of the order of 1-5 per cent) limits the direct anti-competitive effect of revenue pooling arrangements, the subsidiary articles of the agreements may also inhibit competition. For example, promotion of the route by either airline may be restricted to promotion that does not discriminate between them or which benefits each airline equally. The net effect of these pooling arrangements is often to reduce competition between the pool partners to a very low level. An important item in the process of negotiating pool agreements is the determination of the pool accounting unit. Transfers of revenue between participating airlines are not based on real yields, as these are not public. Instead, both airlines set up together a "notional" yield, generally based on the previous year's average income, and calculate each participant's notional revenue by multiplying passengers by this standard unit. As passengers numbers are easily checked, such a system is relatively easy to enforce. But it is the most anticompetitive aspect of airline cooperation. As each airline's share is calculated using notional yields, discounting fares does not reduce an airline's share in the revenue pool; an airline discounting, on average, more

than its partner is penalized, as it may have to transfer excess revenue which it did not earn. Therefore capacity and revenue pooling agreements discourage airlines very strongly from offering low fares.

D. MOTIVES AND EFFECTS OF REGULATION

1. The rationale for regulation of passenger air transport

89.   There would appear to be a number of major reasons for the extensive international and national regulation of air transport described above. Once the 1944 Chicago Convention had established the principle of each country's sovereignty over its own territory there was the evident need for procedures to regulate the use of that air space by foreign as well as domestic carriers - hence the framework of bilateral agreements and other internationally agreed rules based on reciprocity which have been described earlier in this chapter.

90.   At the national level, there would appear to be three main reasons for government intervention. Firstly, the public service nature of air transport has been advanced to ensure that there was a regular and reliable provision of air services to all parts of the country at the lowest cost consistent with a reasonable return to the carriers. Thus scheduled services therefore required protection from charter services since the former could not withdraw services but were committed to operating them whether the aircraft was full or not. Regulation is thus seen as providing stability and ensuring a profitable industry. Also protective regulation has been pursued to ensure that some services can cross-subsidise others.

91.   Secondly, the relatively small size of most domestic markets was considered as not being able to support free competition which would lead to inadequate service or destructive competition. It is argued that the industry has a homogeneous product and relative ease of entry, which could lead to new entrants undercutting incumbents' tariffs and hence to a price war. Alternatively, in some countries, the view was held that the industry had natural monopoly characteristics so that regulation was justified to prevent excessive pricing.

92.   Thirdly, and related to the first two, it was believed on public policy grounds that the industry should remain under domestic control as a vital national resource and hence there was a need for extensive public involvement in airlines through direct public ownership of airlines as well as by government regulation of entry and exit, capacity and tariffs.

93.   As regards airline pooling agreements, it has been argued that these are necessary to give an incentive to airlines to operate outside profitable (peak) periods, to improve load factors as well as to contribute to a more efficient use of aircraft and airports. For the consumer, it is argued that cooperation between airlines in the form of pooling agreements enables the consumer to benefit from the interline system.

2. The effects of regulation

94.   The scope of regulation of air transport, particularly the international regulations, has a number of consequences for airlines in relation to their ability to compete.

95.   In the first place, there is considerable restriction on their freedom of access to particular markets. Entry requires government support to the extent that bilateral agreements are required for international services, for obtaining traffic rights and for determining the routes that may be operated. This requires either the negotiation of a new bilateral agreement or renegotiation of an existing one. The other country may not wish for a change or may exact a high price for any change. For example, to obtain fifth freedom rights and sometimes even for third and fourth freedom rights, airlines may be required to pay royalties.

96.   Secondly, the level of output of each airline is not at its own discretion. Its production may be limited through bilateral agreements on capacity control or on equal sharing of capacity, or through inter-airline agreements on revenue sharing and capacity. An airline wishing to increase its capacity and output on routes where there is some form of bilateral or inter-airline capacity control may well find that the other airline in the duopoly may be unable or unwilling to increase its own capacity, and therefore may veto the expansion plans. Capacity limitations are widespread but have not existed in all markets. On many routes to or from the United States there was little effective capacity control even before deregulation.

97.   Finally, airlines' pricing freedom is also limited. This is partly because most tariffs have traditionally been set by the IATA tariffs conferences in which the influence of any individual airline was limited and partly because governments had to approve all tariffs. Thus, even on routes where IATA tariffs do not apply or where IATA now allows innovatory tariffs by the third and fourth freedom carriers concerned, the government at either end of the route may prevent a new fare being introduced. Even non-IATA airlines are required by governments to apply IATA tariffs on most of their international routes. Pricing freedom has only existed in markets where at times there has been widespread discounting of IATA tariffs or in markets where with the connivance of governments the IATA tariffs process has been abandoned. This has been the case on most of the North Atlantic and trans-Pacific routes to and from the United States since about 1978. With these major exceptions airline managers have not been free to choose and set their own tariffs at will. Tariffs have had to be approved by IATA or by the two governments concerned. In practice such approvals have depended on the agreement of the other airline(s) on the route in question. Pricing freedom was further restricted if airlines were in revenue pools with the other carriers.

98.   In addition to the competitive constraints on airlines, there are a number of costs of operating the present regulatory framework for air transport resulting from the absence of effective competition. These concern chiefly the levels of tariffs and profits obtained by airlines. In markets where there is price competition, tariffs are more likely to reflect the levels at which the more efficient carriers can operate profitably. Tariffs arrived at through inter-airline negotiations must inevitably be a compromise between the pricing policies of the high-cost and those of the low-cost

airlines. This is what has happened within IATA. As a result the IATA tariffs appear to have been based less on the costs of the more efficient carriers and more on the projected costs of the higher cost operators.

99.   Prior to 1979, the unanimity rule at IATA tariff conferences resulted in negotiations between participants in order to achieve unanimity among airlines with very diverse cost levels. This resulted in very different fares for routes with similar cost characteristics. This was so even after 1979 when the unanimity rule was effectively abandoned. On many routes factors such as surface competition, or competition from charters, may have a more profound effect on tariffs than traffic density, sector length or other cost factors.

100.   The wide variation in fares on routes which are outwardly similar suggests that there is considerable cross-subsidization between routes, and even between different classes of passengers on the same route. One significant effect on consumer interests in general is that it holds back the development of air services in growth markets because they may be burdened with unusually high fares.

101.   In this context it is interesting to compare intra-European and domestic US traffic, the former amounting to about half of the latter in terms of passengers. This difference cannot be explained by the size of population in both areas, a comparison which would make the contrast even stronger, nor by differences in per capita GNP which are not significant. The existence of intermodal competition (air v. rail) is certainly a strong factor in Europe. Other elements such as high operating costs which contribute to increased fares can be enumerated but these factors are not exogeneous to the performance of the airlines concerned and the market conditions under which they operate. It may well be that the relatively small size of the European air market is partly due to regulatory constraints and once these constraints are eased the market will expand rapidly.

102.   The absence of effective price competition in most airline markets has had two adverse effects. It has meant higher costs than would have been the case in a more competitive environment because it has reduced the incentive to cut costs. Higher tariffs have also encouraged the growth of low fare charters.

103.   As regards airlines' profits, on routes where an effective duopoly exists and where the duopolists are operating in a revenue-sharing pool, or where capacity is controlled and equally shared on the basis of the air services agreement, the carriers involved have been in a position to extract monopoly profits. They have done this by effectively controlling the provision of capacity and by controlling fare levels through the IATA traffic conference or inter-airline agreements. In practice, this has meant unusually high fare levels and high load factors. It is significant to note the results of a study of partial liberalisation of the UK domestic market in this context (see also Chapter 4 below) which found that the major effect on prices that liberalisation seems to have brought about is a one-off (relative) reduction in the economy price at the time of entry of a new carrier whereas longer term price competition seems to be confined to discount fares. The results of deregulation in the United States have also generally shown considerable benefits to consumers in terms of lower fares, flight frequency and travel times.

CHAPTER III

APPLICATION OF COMPETITION LAWS AND POLICIES
TO PASSENGER AIR TRANSPORT

A. OVERVIEW

104.   In all OECD countries providing information, the air transport sector is subject to some degree of exemption from the full force of applicable national competition laws, mainly for the reason that the sector is subject to other overriding forms of national or international regulation. The scope of this exemption however varies considerably from one country to another. At the one extreme, there are two countries where the sector is totally exempted -- Ireland (this exemption was removed by amending legislation adopted late in 1987) and Portugal. At the other, there is one country -- the United States -- where there are very few exemptions which are narrowly circumscribed so that particularly since the beginning of airline deregulation in 1978 almost all activities in the sector have been subject to the antitrust laws. Most countries evidently lie somewhere between these two extremes. Most commonly, exemptions exist or may be available in a number of countries for agreements between carriers relating to government approved tariffs, schedules or other operating conditions. On the other hand, mergers or abuses of dominant positions are usually subject to control even though this may sometimes be exercised jointly by the competition and aviation authorities.

105.   In practice, where they are applicable, there would appear to have been relatively few cases of national competition laws being applied to passenger air transport. Six countries -- Belgium, Japan, the Netherlands, Finland, Norway and Spain -- reported no formal cases, although in Japan, in 1986 a warning was issued to three air carriers in relation to a suspected agreement on discounts to certain groups of passengers.

106.   Of the cases reported in the remaining countries, most concerned discriminatory discount arrangements or mergers.

107.   Since the April 1986 Court of Justice ruling in the Nouvelles Frontières case which confirmed the applicability of the EEC rules of competition to the airline sector, there has been an intensification of the attempts by the EEC Commission to inject more competition into European air services. In particular, the Commission asked all the major European airlines to modify their agreements with one another so as to eliminate the most serious distortions of competition such as extensive revenue pooling, capacity sharing and fare agreements. In addition, on 14th December, the Council of Transport Ministers of the European Communities agreed upon a set of Commission proposals designed to liberalise air transport as well as to bring

the sector fully within the rules of competition by adopting a procedural regulation applying Articles 85 and 86 to air transport as well as a block exemption for certain categories of agreements and concerted practices.

108.   The following paragraphs give a country-by-country survey of the way competition laws are presently applied to air transport.

B. REVIEW BY COUNTRY

109.   In **Australia**, section 51(1) of the Trade Practices Act provides statutory exemption for activities specifically authorised by Commonwealth, State or Territory legislation or any regulation made under such legislation. The economic regulation of domestic aviation occurs mainly through three pieces of Federal legislation passed in 1981: the Airlines Agreement Act, which provides for consultations and agreement between the two domestic Australian airlines, in particular in relation to aircraft utilisation, load factors and fares; the Airlines Equipment Act, which regulates capacity; and the Independent Air Fares Committee Act which established an independent statutory authority to determine and approve air fares charged for all scheduled domestic air services with the exception of intrastate services.

110.   Although case law is unsettled on the scope of this exemption, the effect of the legislation is to largely exempt the provision of trunk route services and domestic air fare-setting from the anti-competitive provisions of the Trade Practices Act.   This situation will markedly change from 1990 when the Government withdraws from the economic regulation of domestic aviation. In the post 1990 deregulated environment, the aviation industry will be fully exposed to the Trade Practices Act.   Any move towards the emergence of a monopoly on the network of national or trunk routes would be dealt with by section 50 of the Act, which covers market dominance resulting from mergers. Other provisions of the Act would prevent the abuse of market power, such as predatory pricing, and other anti-competitive practices.

111.   With regard to international aviation, there are jurisdictional limitations to the application of the Act but it may apply, and has been applied, in certain cases.   One such case involved an application by IATA for authorisation of certain arrangements insofar as they applied to the activities of member airlines operating in Australia.   Under the Trade Practices Act, the Trade Practices Commission may authorise on public benefit grounds some arrangements which are, on the face of it, anti-competitive.

112.   The arrangements for which IATA sought authorisation related to client services, interlining, certain agency matters, and tariff co-ordination.   In December 1985, the Commission authorised these arrangements.   It found that there was public benefit in IATA's non-tariff arrangements as they contributed to the efficient operation of international airline services to and from Australia.

113.   The Commission also found that there was public benefit in the tariff co-ordination arrangements.   While acknowledging that arrangements to co-ordinate and compile tariffs reflects a consensus or agreement by the participating airlines, the subsequent availability of IATA tariff information provides a basis for determining fares and fare structures that is known

throughout the industry, with price competition determining actual fares according to market conditions.

114.   Originally, IATA had sought authorisation for certain arrangements to enforce compliance with IATA tariffs and to restrict advertising of fares actually offered by airlines. The Commission refused to authorise these tariff compliance arrangements as they would preclude competitive pricing or discounting of fares in Australia. However, the tariff co-ordination arrangements authorised by the Commission in December 1985 did not include any compliance machinery and allowed room for competition in prices and discounts.

115.   In **Belgium**, the Act of 27th May 1960 on protection against the abuse of economic power is applicable to air transport. However it does not override the specific national laws and regulations that have been adopted in the air transport sector nor international agreements regulating air transport (schedules, lines, aircraft capacity, tariffs, etc.).

116.   In **Canada**, the Competition Act of 1986 is a law of general application establishing rules for fair and effective competition in the Canadian economy. Its prohibitions, however, do not apply where valid legislation authorises behaviour considered to be in the public interest with respect to specific industries. The leading case with respect to the application of Canadian competition laws to regulated industries is the decision of the Supreme Court of Canada in B.C. Law Society v. Jabour (1982). The applicability of the Competition Act in industries subject to regulatory oversight is, by that decision, residual and has application only to such activities which are not affected by the exercise of the powers conferred on the regulator. It should be noted however, that the Jabour decision was rendered under the Combines Investigation Act and in the context of criminal law enforcement. The Competition Act now provides for extensive review of business practices by the Competition Tribunal pursuant to civil law jurisdiction. In this latter context, it remains to be determined to what extent the Jabour decision will apply.

117.   The laws concerning the economic regulation of commercial air services in Canada, domestic and international, are contained in the federal National Transportation Act, 1967. A major overhaul of this legislation was adopted by Parliament in 1987 and came into force on January 1, 1988. This revised Act reflects the first major sectoral application of the Canadian government's general regulatory reform policy, announced in April 1986, by the Deputy Prime Minister. It incorporates a philosophy of less regulation, greater reliance on competition and market forces and a more open and accessible regulatory regime.

118.   This new legislation will result in effective deregulation of domestic southern air services allowing for open entry by carriers and considerable pricing flexibility subject only to regulatory review of unreasonable price increases in non-competitive markets. Although Canada's Northern and remote areas, which account for 2 per cent of total airline revenues, will also be subject to regulatory reform, limited economic regulation will continue in these regions of Canada due to the economic fragility of these services and because of the greater dependency northerners have on the regular provision of air services. This regulation will include a reverse onus public interest entry test and more extensive rate review than is the case for Southern Canada.

119.   However, the new legislation will not substantially change the manner in which international air services are regulated. A new international air policy was announced by the Minister of Transport on October 2, 1987. It will introduce competition and flexibility to this sector. International air fares are always formally subject to review by the countries negotiating the bilateral agreements, but the recent agreement between Canada and the United Kingdom demonstrated Canada's commitment to price competition.

120.   With respect to both domestic and international air services, the National Transportation Act provides for the review of mergers and acquisitions of federally regulated air carriers. The legislation is intended to ensure that changes in ownership of transportation businesses do not jeopardize the objectives of the national Transportation Policy. The Act, however, contains specific sections which state that these regulatory provisions do not affect the application of other Acts of Parliament. The merger provisions of the Competition Act would therefore apply concurrently to mergers and acquisitions in the airline industry.

121.   There have been no significant competition law cases involving the air transport industry, due largely to the regulatory regime in which air carriers have to date operated. The defence to the Competition Act afforded to regulated activities has however, been held not to extend to the advertising practices of air carriers [Regina v. Air Canada (1987), Ontario District court, unreported. Notice of appeal has been filed]. It is anticipated that to the extent that the provisions of the National Transportation Act, 1987, ease the regulatory regime in which air carriers operate, the circumstances under which the Competition Act will have application will be correspondingly increased.

122.   On a number of occasions the Director of Investigation and Research (Director), under authority of section 27.1 of the Combines Investigation Act, now section 97 of the Competition Act, intervened in Canadian Transport Commission (CTC) hearings in order to introduce evidence and deliver arguments favouring a pro-competitive approach to regulation. These interventions included appearances in support of individual applications for authority to operate as well as representations dealing with more general policy issues.

123.   A major intervention took place in April 1984 when the Air Transport Committee of the CTC held hearings to examine fare regulation as well as general economic regulation in the domestic air carrier industry. The Director's submission at these hearings relied on the beneficial results of air deregulation in the United States in advocating similar regulatory reform in Canada. However, the CTC, in its Interim Report, recommended that deregulation should continue, although on a more relaxed basis. This mixed recommendation went on to call for increased flexibility on discount fare offerings, and for more weight to be given to the benefits of competition in deliberations respecting public convenience and necessity. It should also be noted that at about the same time, the Minister of Transport introduced measures to deregulate aspects of the industry so as to encourage competitive entry and price flexibility. This policy initiative was ultimately realized in the provisions of the National Transportation Act, 1987.

124.   In **Denmark**, according to Section 2(2) of the Monopolies and Restrictive Practices Supervision Act 1955 as amended (the Monopolies Act),

the Act does not apply to "price conditions or business activities which, under special authorisation, are determined or approved by public authorities".

125.   Air transport is regulated by Statute No.252 of 10th June 1960 on civil aviation as amended, which is administered by the Ministry of Public Services (the Ministry of Transport).

126.   In 1961, the Monopolies Appeal Tribunal made a decision to the effect that the exemption rule in Section 2(2) of the Monopolies Act did not apply to the conditions laid down in the IATA Resolution No.810 for acceptance of sales agents and payment of commissions, as these conditions had not been approved by the Ministry of Transport.

127.   Furthermore, the Appeal Tribunal determined that the 12 IATA airlines which had no independent agency in Denmark were under an obligation, according to Section 6(2) of the Monopolies Act, to notify these IATA conditions, to which they were bound, to the register of the Monopolies Control Authority (MCA).

128.   After introduction of the "International Agreement on the Procedure for the Establishment of Scheduled Air Services" of 10th July 1967, which Denmark joined on 15th March 1972, the competence and control of the IATA Resolution was transferred to the Ministry of Transport. Consequently, the MCA cancelled the registration of IATA in 1985.

129.   In May 1969, the Danish travel agency Tjaereborg Rejser and the charter company Sterling Airways lodged a complaint with the MCA, because travel agents who had contracts for charter flights with the charter airline Scanair, which is a sister company of SAS, had special favours in the form of discounts of about 50 per cent on connecting flights by SAS ordinary domestic services to and from the point of departure of the charter flight. Subsequently, the complaint was expanded to comprise connecting flights on inter Scandinavian routes as well.

130.   The MCA found that the Monopolies Act was applicable to the case, as it concerned terms of prices and discounts which were not determined or approved by the Ministry of Transport.

131.   The special discount arrangement, which had been implemented in 1967, was terminated on 1st November 1970. At the same time the travel agency Scandinavian Startour Corporation (SSC), which also includes the Danish travel agency Stjernerejser, got a clearing arrangement for connecting flights on SAS-served routes, which has the same effect as the cancelled discount arrangement. This arrangement was terminated on 1st October 1971, after SAS had become a principal partner of the SSC.

132.   The MCA found during the case that it was a question of unreasonable discount discrimination in violation of Section 11(1) of the Monopolies Act. But as the arrangement had been finally terminated as from 1st October 1971, the MCA found no reason to intervene.

133.   In **Finland**, the Act on the promotion of economic competition of 1973, as amended, is in principle applicable to the air transport sector but the Act does not override the special national legislation or international agreements regulating air transport.

134.   In **France**, the rules of competition (formerly the Ordinance of 30th June 1945, now replaced by the Ordinance of 1st December 1986) apply to air transport.

135.   These rules prohibit concerted actions, practices or agreements which prevent, restrict or distort competition.   However, those practices the authors of which can justify that they have the effect of ensuring economic progress and that the practices confer on users a fair share of the benefits which result from such practices without giving to the enterprises involved the possibility of eliminating competition for a substantial part of the products in question are exempted from the prohibition as are those practices "which result from the application of a law or regulation".

136.   It is this latter provision for exemption which has allowed national and international scheduled air transport services to enjoy up to the present time a special position which is evidenced both by the national regulations applicable to the sector as well as by international bilateral and multinational agreements on international air services.

137.   These exemptions do however have a number of conditions attached to them which are laid down in the regulations mentioned above, such as the requirement that French and foreign airlines must obtain approval of the services and tariffs which they intend to put into effect.   This allows the authorities to ensure that capacities and tariffs correspond to the public's needs.

138.   The promulgation of the new Competition Ordinance and the elaboration of a Community regulation to apply specifically the rules of competition of the Treaty of Rome to the air transport sector have brought about a rethinking of the existing framework.   Thus, henceforth, practices between companies engaged in operating intra-Community air services will no longer enjoy immunity from the application of the rules of competition unless they satisfy certain specific criteria.   This cannot fail to have repercussions on other aspects of international air transport.

139.   In **Germany**, Section 99(1) of the Act against Restraints of Competition (ARC) exempts restrictive agreements, decisions and recommendations of transport enterprises and of the associations of such enterprises from all provisions of the ARC if and insofar as they refer to tariffs and conditions of transport services and connected services established or approved under an act or ordinance.

140.   Flight schedules, tariffs and conditions of scheduled air transport require governmental approval (Section 21 of the Air Traffic Act -- Luftverkehrsgesetz) and are therefore exempted from the ARC, just like government-approved take-off, landing and airport charges (Section 43 of the Air Traffic Licensing Ordinance -- Luftverkehrs-Zulassungsordnung).   The exemption from the ARC of specific governmental measures reflects the legislative intent of permitting state interference with free competition in the transport sector.   However, the Federal Cartel Office (FCO) is examining the 1987 summer flight tariffs of Lufthansa from the EEC competition rules point of view to determine whether they result from concerted practices. Landing and other airport charges are also subject to scrutiny under the EEC competition rules to ensure that concerted practices or discrimination are not involved.

141. Where airlines and airport enterprises and associations of such enterprises, in connection with border-crossing transport, engage in restrictive practices not requiring governmental approval according to Section 99(2), Nos.1 and 2, they are exempt from the ban on cartels (Section 1 of the ARC), as well as the provisions on resale price maintenance (Section 15 of the ARC) and restrictions on distribution (Section 18 of the ARC). However, the exempted practices are subject to abuse supervision by the competition authorities (Section 104 of the ARC).

142. Except for government-approved tariffs and conditions, in particular flight schedules, airline tariffs and airport charges, the ARC is applicable to air transport either under the special provision regulating the supervision of abuses of the air transport exemption (Section 104) or unrestrictedly.

143. Mergers to which air carriers are parties are subject to merger control by the FCO (Sections 23 et seq. of the ARC). The air transport markets are comparatively highly concentrated, not least as a result of the governmental air transport policy. Mergers, and in particular mergers to which the national German airline Lufthansa is a party and which result in a strengthening of the latter's position on the air transport markets, may meet the requirements for prohibition specified in the merger control provisions (Section 24 of the ARC). To give an example, in 1981, the FCO prohibited Deutsche Lufthansa AG from acquiring a stake in a major group of travel agencies (F.i.r.s.t.) on the grounds that Lufthansa's paramount market position in respect of air package tours would be further strengthened as a result of the merger.

144. A further area where competition law is applied to air transport is the ban on discrimination (Section 26(2) of the ARC). Insofar as airlines are powerful enterprises, they are caught by the ban on discrimination, for instance when concluding agency contracts with travel agents. In several proceedings, the FCO has used its influence to the effect that such contracts are concluded on the basis of objective and factually justified criteria; formal decisions have so far not been made, though.

145. The German ban on discrimination moreover grants every aggrieved enterprise a civil law right to sue dominant and powerful enterprises which resort to treatment that is unjustifiably different from that accorded to similar enterprises (Section 35 in connection with Section 26(2) of the ARC). In a civil suit, for example, the Federal Supreme Court held discriminatory commission payments to a travel agency by IATA air carriers to violate the ban on discrimination.

146. Other ARC provisions have so far not gained importance in FCO cases involving air transport.

147. In **Greece**, Section 5 of the Act No.703/77 on the control of monopolies and oligopolies and the protection of free competition provides for the application of the Act to public undertakings or to undertakings serving the public interest. However, the Ministers of National Economy and Commerce may, by joint decision, exempt from the application of this Act certain of these enterprises if they are of general importance to the national economy. Since Olympic Airways has not been exempted, the provisions of this Act are applied.

148.   In **Ireland**, until the adoption of amending legislation in 1987, domestic competition laws did not apply to air services or services ancillary thereto. However, the new amending legislation passed late in 1987 has removed this exemption.

149.   In **Japan**, the Antimonopoly Act is generally applicable to the air transport sector.

150.   However, as regards agreements between air carriers, in accordance with the Aviation Act, the Act does not apply to legitimate conduct which is authorised by the Minister of Transport, provided that unfair trade practices are not employed or that fares and charges are not excessively enhanced through substantially restraining competition in any particular field of trade.

151.   There have been no decisions for violation of the Antimonopoly Act. However, when the Ministry of Transport adopted a flexible approval procedure for reduced fares, there was a suspicion that the three domestic air carriers had concertedly agreed upon certain conditions in advance (increasing the discount rate applied to fares for groups of tourists, etc.). The Fair Trade Commission investigated the three carriers and, in August 1986, issued a warning to the enterprises concerned.

152.   In the **Netherlands**, the Economic Competition Act is applicable to the air transport sector. However, agreements in the sector of international transport, including air transport, to which one or some foreign enterprises are party, have been exempted from the obligation to notify. This does not preclude the application of the Act to such agreements but, in practice, there have been no cases of enforcement of the Act against restrictive agreements or dominant positions in the air transport sector.

153.   In **New Zealand**, civil aviation is subject to the general competition law, the Commerce Act 1986. However, it was recognised that a potential conflict existed between New Zealand competition law and the extra-territorial limits on the jurisdiction of domestic laws in relation to bilateral agreements. A transitional exception from the provisions of the Commerce Act was therefore provided for international carriage by air generally until 1st March 1987. From that date, the Civil Aviation Act 1964 was amended to permit on the one hand, international aviation contracts, arrangements or understandings relating to tariffs and/or capacity, and on the other, international air tarrifs per se, to be authorised under that Act for the purposes of exemption from the Commerce Act. Such authorisations may be granted only after regard has been paid to New Zealand government policies on external aviation and international obligations, plus other specified criteria. For example, in the case of tariffs-related contracts, arrangements or understandings, provisions which unjustifiably discriminate between consumers, exclude any other supplier from participating in the market or prevent their offering other tariffs could preclude authorisation under the amended Act. Similarly in the case of actual tariffs filed for authorisation, these specific criteria include whether the proposed tariff is excessive in terms of a reasonable return on investment by the supplier; whether the supply of carriage at that tariff can be carried on for a reasonable period; and whether consumers generally or a significant group is likely to benefit substantially.

154. The Commerce Commission is responsible for the enforcement of the various prohibitions contained in the Commerce Act. The Commission is also able to authorise certain exemptions from the Act on public benefit grounds, and is responsible for clearing or authorising mergers and takeovers. There is also provision for private actions for damages to be taken by persons affected by any restrictive trade practice prohibited by the Act. However, in the case of international aviation, the new competition related provisions of the Civil Aviation Act 1964 are administered by the Air Services Policy Division of the Ministry of Transport, with the power to authorise tariffs and/or capacity related agreements etc., and specific tariffs, for the purposes of exemption from the Commerce Act vested in the Minister of Civil Aviation and Meteorological Services.

155. In **Portugal**, the air transport sector has not yet been brought within the scope of the Act No 422/83 of 3rd December 1983 on the Protection of Competition. Section 36(3) of the Act requires the Government to determine by special regulation the conditions under which the Act will apply to transport generally. No regulation has yet been issued.

156. In **Norway**, the competition laws apply in principle to aviation. However, no significant cases have arisen since the establishment of SAS in 1951.

157. In **Spain**, the Act No 110/63 is applicable to air transport except in cases where restrictions to competition are laid down in specific legal provisions.

158. In **Sweden**, the Competition Act is applicable to restraints of trade occasioned by air transport enterprises with effects on the Swedish market. For enforcement purposes, however, it is necessary here to comply with special rules. Where restraints of trade are of the kind which are a necessary or intended consequence of public regulation, they cannot under the Competition Act be deemed contrary to the public interest. Insofar as regulation as such or its application takes on inappropriate trade-restraining effects, the Competition Ombudsman (NO) is empowered under his official instructions (as indicated by statements in the Government Bill which led to the Competition Act) to take steps to ensure the avoidance of acts which curtail competition unnecessarily. Under the terms of this governmental mandate, NO is also asked to examine different forms of barriers to business entry that might be detrimental to competition.

159. By way of illustrating the aviation question, mention can be made of a case that was finally settled in 1973 after decision taken by the Market Court (MD). This concerned the practice of SAS of granting discounts on feeder flights to connecting journeys operated by Scanair, a charter airline belonging to the same group of companies as SAS. According to MD, the risk might arise here of adverse effects on competitors in the pursuit of their trade as well as on efficiency and price formation in the charter sector. But by the time MD heard this case, the granting of discounts had been discontinued, which meant that there was no longer any question of discrimination.

160. In **Switzerland**, the competition legislation applies to all types of restrictions affecting Switzerland irrespective of the economic sectors in which they occur.

161.   In the **United Kingdom**, the competition legislation applies in general to air transport but various aspects of air transport are excluded or exempted from purview.

162.   Competition matters relating to international airline services (other than charter flights) are excluded from the scope of both the Competition Act 1980 and the monopoly provisions of the Fair Trading Act 1973. [See Schedule 1 of the Anti-Competitive Practices (Exclusions) Order 1980, as amended by the Anti-Competitive Practices (Exclusions) (Amendments) Order 1984, and Schedule 7 of the Fair Trading Act 1973, as amended by the Monopoly References (Alteration of Exclusions) Order 1984.]

163.   Agreements (a) to which the only parties are air transport undertakings; and (b) between air transport undertakings and their agents, under which the only restrictions accepted are in respect of carriage by air, are excluded from the scope of the Restrictive Trade Practices Act 1976. [See the Schedule to the Restrictive Trade Practices (Services) Order 1976.]

164.   In 1985, the Director General of Fair Trading gained additional powers under the Fair Trading Act 1973 and the Competition Act 1980 to enable him to play a greater part in the support of the Civil Aviation Authority in matters affecting airline competition. An agreed statement, explaining how the Director General's new powers complemented those of the Authority, was published in the Authority's "Official Record" in May 1985. This concordat explained that while the Director General could initiate action on competition matters in civil aviation (other than those that are concerned with international scheduled airline services), it was expected that complaints about anti-competitive behaviour would usually be considered first by the Civil Aviation Authority.

165.   In 1986 the Civil Aviation Authority heard an application by Britannia Airways which was designed to place limits on the participation by British Airways and its subsidiary British Airtours in the short-haul leisure market in general and in the inclusive tour charter market in particular. This was a complex case but the essence of it was Britannia's claim that British Airways' size and strength, its domination of international scheduled services and its privileged position at Heathrow gave it the opportunity to exploit these advantages to compete unfairly with specialist charter airlines. The Authority refused the application because it saw no evidence of any behaviour by British Airways which was inconsistent with the objectives of the Civil Aviation Act. The Secretary of State for Transport upheld this decision on appeal but asked the Authority to review certain aspects of the case. The Authority wrote to representatives and users in the industry and other interested parties in January 1987 seeking their views on, inter alia, how it should distinguish between vigorous and legitimate competitive behaviour and illegimate anti-competitive behaviour, whether it needed additional information to enable it to deal with such behaviour and whether the timescales against which such matters can be effectively dealt with needed to or could be adjusted.

166.   The merger provisions of the Fair Trading Act 1973 do apply to the air transport sector and in August 1987, the Secretary of State for Trade and Industry referred the proposed acquisition by British Airways Plc of British Caledonian Group Plc to the Monopolies and Mergers Commission (MMC). In

November 1987, the MMC reported that the acquisition might be expected not to operate against the public interest.

167. The Commission identified a number of possible detrimental effects of the acquisition. It was noted that the removal of competition between BA and BCAL would leave some routes on which there would be little competition for the merged airline; that the airline would occupy a very powerful market position; that it might present a threat to charter operators at Gatwick; and that it might withhold from competing airlines maintenance, repairs and training facilities at present provided to them by BCAL.

168. A number of possible benefits were also identified. The merger would strengthen BA's ability to compete with major foreign airlines world wide; it would bring financial savings through the merger of activities and financial benefits or synergy; and it would have the consequence of removing whatever risk there might be of the enforced liquidation of BCG - which faced financial difficulties - or the breaking up of its business.

169. In order to diminish the detrimental effects, BA proposed inter alia: to return all BCAL's licences to operate domestic routes and certain foreign routes to the Civil Aviation Authority; to withdraw BCAL's pending appeals against the CAA granting Air Europe licences to certain routes; that BA would not oppose any application made at any time for a licence by another airline to operate in competition with the merged airline; that the merged airline would operate as one carrier for the purpose of designation on international routes; that BA would submit for review by the CAA all routes at present operated by BCAL, for the purpose of seeing whether further British competition would be desirable; that BA would surrender a minimum of 5,000 slots at Gatwick, spread throughout the year; BA would continue to offer to other airlines without discrimination the maintenance and repair facilities at present made available to other airlines by BCAL; and BA would merge the charter activities of British Airtours with the small activities operated by BCAL under the BCAL name.

170. The MMC considered that the possible effect of the merger on competition would be reduced very considerably by these proposals through the return of licences and slots (nearly 20,000 slots at Gatwick if none of the licences to be returned is reissued to BA). The position of the merged airline at Gatwick would be modified considerably and opportunities for the growth and development of other airlines would be correspondingly increased. The proposed merger also led to complaints being made to the European Commission in respect of possible breaches of the competition rules of the Community. These complaints are not yet resolved.

171. After the BA bid was cleared by the MMC a rival bid from SAS was launched. This bid was not sent for investigation by the MMC as the Secretary of State for Trade and Industry did not believe that significant competition issues arose from the bid. (In the event SAS's bid was unsuccessful.)

172. In the **United States**, competition laws and policies apply to aviation. There are three exceptions. First, carriers may submit to the Department of Transportation (DOT) any agreement they reach and ask DOT to approve it and grant it immunity from the antitrust laws. This authority has been very sparingly used since deregulation. Second, mergers among air carriers must be submitted to DOT and may not be consummated unless DOT

approves them. The substantive standard contained in the law governing airline mergers, however, is virtually the same as that contained in the antitrust laws. Third, agreements among carriers affecting international aviation may be submitted to the Department of Transportation and may be immunised from the antitrust laws. The first two exceptions are scheduled, under current law, to terminate as of 31st December 1988. The Administration has submitted legislation that would advance those termination dates. The third exception will remain in place indefinitely.

173. In the period 1985 to 1987, six major acquisition cases came before the DOT, in three of which the Department of Justice opposed DOT approval on the grounds that they were anticompetitive. Five of these mergers were allowed to proceed while the sixth - USAir and Piedmont - is pending in the US Court of Appeals.

174. In April 1985, **United Airlines** offered to buy **Pan American's** Pacific Division. The Department of Justice (DOJ) filed a brief stating that they were opposed to the transaction unless United agreed to spin off one gateway to Tokyo from the West Coast of the United States. With a reduction in the number of US carriers in the Pacific from three to two (Northwest Airlines was also a carrier), and with the restrictions on entry and capacity dictated by the US-Japan bilaterals, DOJ felt the transfer would strengthen the IATA fare cartel.

175. The Department of Transportation agreed that there might be some loss of competition due to the transfer, but felt that it was not likely to be substantial. In particular, they pointed to a new Memorandum of Understanding between the United States and Japan that would allow new entry in the Pacific market in 1986. DOT also agreed to authorise a future proceeding to determine if another carrier should be chosen to replace United in the Seattle-Tokyo market. Subsequently, and in keeping with the Memorandum of Understanding, American Airlines, Delta Airlines, and a new Japanese Carrier (ANA) were given gateways to Tokyo.

176. **Northwest Airlines** filed an application with DOT in January 1986 for permission to merge with **Republic Airlines**. Both carriers had major hub operations in Minneapolis and were head-to-head competitors on 45 city pairs. The combined carrier would control 80 per cent of the gates at the Minneapolis airport. There was also substantial competition between the two airlines in Detroit. The Department of Justice opposed the acquisition on the grounds that it was likely to reduce competition in non-stop city-pair markets to and from Minneapolis. There are substantial economies in running a complete hub operation. DOJ argued that for a new carrier to discipline the market power of the combined airline it would have to enter with a complete hub operation. The Department felt that this was unlikely even in the face of increased fares on the part of Northwest-Republic. DOT disagreed, concluding that the markets cited by DOJ received sufficient competition from one-stop service, connecting service, new entrants, and other forms of service.

177. **TWA** and **Ozark** applied for permission to merge in March 1986, soon after the Northwest/Republic application. The competitive issues in the TWA acquisition were quite similar to those in the Northwest acquisition. Both TWA and Ozark had substantial hub operations at St. Louis, with the combined carriers controlling 76 per cent of the gates. Again the Department of Justice focussed on nonstop city pairs from the hub as being the markets in

which anticompetitive results might occur after the merger. DOJ reiterated the point that there was little chance of entry because of a need for a hub. Their position was that ten gates should be spun off at the St. Louis airport to allow new entry. The Transportation Department disagreed again and approved the merger in September 1986.

178.   The competition issues raised in the takeover of **Eastern Airlines** by **Texas Air** (which owned New York Air) were substantially different from the concerns in the earlier mergers between carriers with overlapping hubs. In this case, the area of substantial concern was competition in the Northeast corridor of the United States. Two routes, Washington–New York and Boston–New York, created special problems. Both routes are heavily dominated by business travellers. Typically, business travellers are time-sensitive and view frequent service as the most important factor in determining which airline to choose. Two airlines, Eastern and New York Air (a Texas Air subsidiary), were direct competitors in these two city pairs for the provision of hourly shuttle service. While other carriers provided irregular service on the two routes, only the merging carriers provided shuttle service between the airports closest to the downtown areas in New York and Washington, as well as at Boston. Thus, there was a substantial possibility that airport pairs represented a relevant market. If so, the proposed combination would have eliminated all existing competition.

179.   The question of whether another carrier would enter the shuttle business in response to the merged carrier's attempt to raise price was complicated in this case because access to the close-in airports, LaGuardia in New York and National in Washington, is restricted. In order to operate at one of these airports a carrier must own a licence, or "slot", that gives them the right to take off or land in a particular hour. Although carriers can buy and sell slots, it was clear that a new carrier contemplating entry would require a substantial number of these slots throughout the day to offer a competitive shuttle service.

180.   To alleviate this problem, and avoid a protracted investigation, Texas Air offered to sell a large number of these slots to Pan American Airways, who would then operate a competing shuttle service. Even so, the Department of Transportation disapproved the transaction, stating that the number of slots offered to Pan Am was not adequate to guarantee a viable shuttle service. Texas Air subsequently resolved these objections by selling Pan Am more slots. The merger was approved on October 1, 1986.

181.   **People Express** was one of the most celebrated examples of deregulation's benefits. The carrier had established a hub at Newark's underutilised airport outside New York City. By offering unrestricted low fares to a large number of locations, the carrier developed a demand for air travel among people who otherwise might not have travelled by air. People Express also showed how new entry could affect the prices of incumbent carriers. However, the airline started to experience significant financial difficulties in early 1986. In September 1986, they agreed to a buyout proposal by **Texas Air**.

182.   People Express operated a hub at Newark, while Texas Air's subsidiary, New York Air did not. Both carriers, however, were carrying primarily local traffic on their routes out of Newark, with People Express generating very little traffic from locations beyond the hub. A lack of beyond traffic is

considered strong evidence that a hub network is not crucial for operating competitive service. This, along with the high density of traffic on the overlapping routes, made entry by a new carrier on a point-to-point basis without a hub likely in response to a price increase by the combined carrier. Thus, any attempt to exercise market power would be kept in check.

183. On October 1, 1986 the Department of Justice conveyed its opinion to the Department of Transportation that "the proposed acquisition is not likely to lessen competition substantially". DOT gave final approval on October 24, 1986.

184. In March 1987, **USAir** offered to acquire **Piedmont Aviation**. Both are East Coast carriers. Although USAir operated primarily in the Northeast and Piedmont operated primarily in the Southeast, there nonetheless was competitive overlap. Both carriers controlled substantial numbers of slots at two capacity-restricted airports, New York's LaGuardia Airport and Washington D.C.'s National Airport. The US Department of Justice concluded that "it could not establish that the merger would eliminate substantial competition". A Phoenix, Arizona-based airline, America West, which was seeking slots at LaGuardia and National, opposed the merger. The US Department of Transportation administrative law judge (ALJ) disapproved the merger because it would increase the two carrier's shares at a number of airports, citing evidence that higher fares were associated with higher shares. DOT reversed the ALJ's decision, rejecting his reading of that evidence, market definition, and evaluation of entry barriers. The case is now pending on appeal in the US Court of Appeals.

185. In the **European Communities**, the European Court of Justice confirmed in the "Nouvelles Frontières" case decided in April 1986 what some national administrations had always denied, namely that the competition rules applied to air transport (1). Executives of airlines and travel agencies including Nouvelles Frontières, Havas, KLM, British Airways and Air France were charged in France with violation of the French Civil Aviation Code when selling air tickets by applying tariffs that had not been submitted to the Minister for Civil Aviation for approval or were different from the approved tariffs. The Court held that it was contrary to the obligations of Member States to approve air tariffs and thus to reinforce the effects thereof where those tariffs were the result of an agreement, a decision by an association of undertakings or a concerted practice.

186. However, the Court also noted that the air transport sector had been excluded from the application of Regulation No.17. Therefore a special procedural regulation was required to enable the Commission to implement effectively Articles 85 and 86 in the air transport sector.

187. The above-mentioned package of liberalisation adopted on 14 December 1987 includes two regulations adopted pursuant to Article 87 of the Treaty (2). The first lays down the procedure for applying the competition rules to air transport. It applies to international air transport between Community airports. This regulation gives the Commission the same powers of investigation and sanction in respect of air transport as it already enjoys in respect of all other sectors of the economy. As in the case of maritime transport, it provides for a 90-day opposition procedure in order to ensure the expeditious treatment of applications for exemption under Article 85(3).

188.   The second regulation enables the Commission to grant block exemptions to various categories of agreement and concerted practice including in particular the joint planning and co-ordination of capacity, the sharing of revenues, consultations on tariffs, fares and conditions, slot allocation and the common purchase, development and operation of computer reservation systems.   These exemptions are to be granted subject to strict conditions whose main purpose is to ensure that competition is neither eliminated nor unduly restricted as a result of the agreements and practices in question. The fares, capacity and access measures referred to in paragraph 84 above are to be revised by the Council by 30 June 1990 and the block exemption will lapse at the end of January 1991.   The Council is committed to adopting further measures of liberalisation with a view to the completion of the internal market in 1992.

189.   In parallel with the negotiations in the Council which led to the adoption of the package, the Commission pursued the proceedings under Article 89 of the EEC Treaty, which it had initiated in 1986, and which it extended in 1987 to embrace also the agreements of the remaining flag-carrying airlines (Iberia, Luxair and TAP).   In a series of meetings with these airlines and in a series of letters sent to them the Commission explained in detail the modifications which would have to be made to their agreements and concerted practices in order to bring them into line with the principles of Article 85.   These modifications were based on the provisions of the block exemption regulation in the form in which it was agreed in principle, so that the Commission's action was fully consistent with the liberalisation package.

190.   Some airlines were initially unwilling to participate in this formal dialogue with the Commission.   The latter therefore proceeded in respect of the agreements between these airlines (Alitalia, Lufthansa and Olympic Airways) to adopt reasoned decisions under Article 89(2) in March 1987. Nevertheless, it gave these airlines a last chance to join the dialogue and when they did so it allowed its decisions (which had not been notified) to lapse.

191.   In the course of the dialogue the airlines agreed to make most of the changes requested by the Commission and informed it that negotiations between them were at an advanced stage.   The Commission, however, was concerned that these changes were not being made sufficiently rapidly.   Following the formal adoption of the package the Commission wrote again to the airlines concerned to inform them that the Article 89 proceedings would lapse with the entry into force of the procedural regulation and that the changes required would now have to be made by 1 January 1988 if the agreements and practices were to qualify for block exemption.

192.   It should also be noted that before the adoption of the new measures, several cases had determined that Regulation No. 17 applies to activities ancillary to air transport such as computer reservation systems, baggage handling and catering services at airports and travel credit cards.   Thus, in 1985, the Commission requested Olympic Airways to supply certain information relating to its costs, market position and implementation of price increases, following a complaint from the Association of Community Airlines that Olympic had abused its dominant position by increasing its charges for handling services by nearly 50 per cent.   Olympic initially refused to supply the information on the grounds that Articles 85 and 86 did not apply to the air transport sector but the Commission held that services ancillary to the

provision of air transport were not covered by the exemption. Olympic Airways subsequently provided the information (3). In another case, the Commission took action against the Belgian airline Sabena to ensure that London European Airways had access to Sabena's computer reservation system SAPHIR. The British company, which began operating a route between Luton and Brussels on 22nd May 1987, had originally been refused access by Sabena to its system which was used for 80 per cent of Belgian reservations (4).

CHAPTER IV

THE MOTIVES FOR DEREGULATION AND ITS EFFECTS

A. THE MOTIVES FOR DEREGULATION AND PRIVATISATION OF PASSENGER AIR
   TRANSPORT

193.   Beginning in the late 1970s and continuing throughout the 1980s there
have been various measures in several OECD countries designed to reduce the
amount of regulation over the air transport sector. The essential motive for
these initiatives was the emerging evidence that the regulatory systems were
inefficient.   They were in fact a costly and often ineffective method of
allocating resources. In the United States, studies into unregulated carriers
operating within individual states showed that these carriers were operating
at lower fares than similar interstate regulated carriers (1).   This chapter
presents a summary of experience with deregulation of US domestic air
transports since 1978, of partial deregulation of UK domestic air transports
since 1976 and an analysis of the effects of one of the more liberal bilateral
agreements, namely that between the Netherlands and the United Kingdom
negotiated in 1984 (2).

194.   As noted in Chapter I, public ownership is widespread in air transport
but in recent years several OECD governments have taken steps towards the
total or partial privatisation of nationally owned airlines. There would seem
to be a variety of reasons for these initiatives, not least the desire to
improve efficiency by subjecting the publicly owned carriers to market
pressures.   Other motives for these moves are the government's desire to
reduce public sector borrowing requirements given the high cost of aircraft
and to allow private capital and management techniques into the industry.
While the process of privatisation is still in its infancy and while there
still remain in all countries strong pressures to retain national control of
air transport, it would seem that privatisation may help the aim of greater
international liberalisation, if governments themselves are not ultimately
responsible for the industry by means of public ownership.

B. EFFECTS OF DEREGULATION IN THE UNITED STATES

1. Routes

195.   Since 1982, entry into US airline markets has been open to all national
carriers that are willing and able to enter. Existing carriers have complete
freedom to abandon or add routes as they see fit. The most significant result
of route deregulation has been the development of hub-and-spoke route
structures.   The economic rationale for hub operations arises from the

54

airlines' ability to take advantage of economies of scope. It may be less costly for a carrier to combine passengers from one city who wish to travel to several destinations onto a single large aircraft through a hub rather than to schedule direct flights between all possible points using smaller planes.

196. Hubbing reduces costs and thereby leads to reduced fares on competitive routes. Hubbing has also allowed airlines to offer connecting one-stop service available on more routes. Although hubbing has eliminated or reduced previously available non-stop service on some routes, it appears that such service was inefficient to provide and was provided only because of inefficient allocations produced by regulation. Following deregulation, such inefficient allocations were eventually discontinued. Some studies have shown that passengers from small communities have benefited from being able to make coordinated connections on one carrier via a hub and that business travellers have benefited from increased flight frequency. Both large and smaller carriers appear to have profited from the hub structure. One open question remains concerning the effect of deregulation on the entry of new carriers. While deregulation has removed the regulatory barriers to entry it may be that hubs could raise the necessary scale to entry in that a carrier may need to develop many "spokes" in order to achieve economies of scope. Although entry into any one city pair appears easy, carriers are operating integrated route networks and thus the viability of any single route is related to the carriers' ability to develop other routes.

2. Fares

197. The consensus in the literature on deregulation is that competition has brought fares more in line with resource costs. Average fares have fallen on long-haul routes, but have risen on short-haul routes. Across all the markets there are various passenger groups that can be considered winners and losers, however. Recent studies by Moore and by Morrison and Winston show that the average unrestricted coach fares have risen, while average discount fares have declined. For example, in their study of 812 city pairs, Morrison and Winston found that coach fares increased 10.3 per cent, while discount fares decreased 15.3 per cent (3). Thus, travellers who continue to fly unrestricted fares have not benefited from deregulation in terms of fares while the vast majority of passengers who pay discount fares have on average benefited. In 1976, prior to deregulation, only 15 per cent of travellers flew on discount fares, by 1987 90 per cent of air passengers took advantage of such fares. According to one study, on average inflation adjusted fares have fallen by 6 per cent notwithstanding a 45 per cent increase in fuel costs that occurred from 1979 to 1985 (4).

198. Although average prices have fallen the comparison between long- and short-haul routes provides a more differentiated picture. Price reductions have mainly occurred in long-distance markets and large-city markets (5). On the other hand, fares have generally increased in small city markets reflecting the higher costs of serving such markets. It must be kept in mind that long-haul travel is significantly more important to passengers than short haul which can be more easily substituted by other forms of transportation. According to Moore's study for example, nearly 90 per cent of passengers were flying long distance.

199. If improvements in flight frequencies as well as fare changes are taken into account, the benefits from deregulation are overwhelmingly positive in the aggregate. Morrison and Winston have estimated that when the changes in fares, flight frequency and time of travel are combined, the total benefit to consumers has been $5.7 billion annually (6). These benefits have been distributed across all markets except the least dense short distance markets.

3. Performance of airlines

200. While a number of airlines were quite successful in absorbing the shock of deregulation and operating in a competitive environment others experienced difficulties of adjustment and a major restructuring of the industry occurred. Indeed, one of the necessary consequences of deregulation is that there must be a possibility that relatively inefficient airlines will lose profitability and go into liquidation. However, on average, available evidence indicates that the airline industry as a whole, as well as consumers, have benefited from deregulation. Although industry earnings fell between 1976 and 1983 most of this decline is attributable to the recession of 1982 and to the increase in real fuel prices during the same period. According to Morris and Winston industry earnings during that period would have been even lower without deregulation (7). Stock market valuations have confirmed the pattern of profitability of the industry. Calculations done by Moore show almost no change in the total value of stock for the big national carriers as a whole in the period between 1976 and 1983 while the market evaluation of regional carriers increased six-fold during the same period (8).

4. Structure of the industry and competition

201. Since deregulation, on an overall nationwide basis the industry has become significantly more concentrated in the United States. The pace of consolidation has been particularly rapid since late 1985 when there were 23 acquisitions by large carriers. However national concentration figures do not capture well the true nature of competition in the industry. Under a widely held view, competition among carriers takes place in the provision of air services between specific city pairs and on average there were more carriers on city pairs than before deregulation.

202. Recently, several studies have been completed to analyse the issue of how market structure affects fares. The general conclusions have been that increases in concentration do lead to increases in fares (9). Thus, the contestable market hypothesis, which states that the actual number of competitors is irrelevant, has been generally rejected.

203. However, there is support for the hypothesis that fares have gradually declined on high density routes into which new and existing firms have entered. Entry of existing large carriers has been found to have an especially large impact on fares on these routes (10). Their ability to match an incumbent carrier's reputation advantage probably explains this phenomenon. In general, the large airlines have not lowered fares as quickly when faced with entry by a low cost airline that promotes itself as a discount carrier. Instead, a two-tier pricing system is usually employed by the large carrier in which lower fares are only available on a fixed number of seats.

204.   Along with the positive economic question of how deregulation has
affected consumer welfare, there are distributional questions of how
deregulation has affected factors of production, i.e. labour and capital. It
appears that deregulation has not had an adverse impact on labour up to this
point. Employment levels are up and average wages have remained relatively
stable. In the long run, however, new carriers not bound by long-term labour
contracts are expected to act as lower cost competitors for the incumbent
airlines, forcing the overall wage level in the industry downward, while
continuing to expand employment.

205.   Changes in the stock market's evaluation of the US carriers since
deregulation clearly shows a strong pattern of winners and losers among
firms.   In general, the two largest full service or trunk carriers (United
Airlines and American Airlines) and the former regional carriers have all
benefited from deregulation in the eyes of the market. The other trunk
carriers have not fared nearly as well in terms of stock market valuation. The
success of a specific set of carriers seems to have been caused primarily by
their ability to utilize effectively route endowments and to preserve
passenger loyalty that they inherited from the regulated period (11).

206.   Three other issues, although closely linked with the allocative and
distributional questions outlined above, are worth mentioning separately.
First, economic deregulation does not appear to have caused a reduction in air
safety standards, which continue to be regulated by the FAA. However, the
changing structure of the industry may require changes in the way safety
regulations are applied, and the type of sanctions that are appropriate. But
there does not seem to be any evidence for a direct link between real
competition between airlines and a reduction in their safety standards.
Second, the US air carriers are now subject fully to all the applicable
antitrust laws. A policy towards mergers set by the Department of
Transportation will have a profound effect on the long-run consequences of
deregulation for competition in air transport. Third, airline computerized
reservation systems (CRS) have become a powerful marketing tool for a few of
the larger carriers. Since a travel agent's reservation is an important input
to the production of air transportation services, it is possible that these
systems could be used to restrict competition. Currently, new rules
promulgated by the Civil Aeronautics Board (CAB) before it ceased operations
at the end of 1984 have placed some restrictions on the ability of carrier
owners of CRS systems to manipulate their systems in an anticompetitive
manner. The Department of Justice reported in December 1985 that the CRS
rules had eliminated most problems of bias. However, the question of monopoly
pricing on access fees remains open, and the Department of Transportation is
currently investigating the issue.

207.   In conclusion, the consequences of deregulation in the US airline
sector appear to be mainly beneficial. There are four main results. First,
the competitive market mechanism has forced a more efficient allocation of
airline resources and an expanded array of price/quality options. Second,
fares have declined on long-haul routes, but increased on short-haul routes.
With the majority of passengers travelling in the longer markets, the average
fare paid has declined. At the same time, business travellers have benefited
from increased flight frequency. Third, stockholders of airlines have
generally benefited, but new employees of the airlines are receiving lower
wages than employees hired previously. Employment, however, has increased.

Last, entry by carriers into other carriers' markets appears to have checked the market power of the incumbent airlines.

C. EFFECTS OF THE PARTIAL DEREGULATION OF THE UNITED KINGDOM AIR TRANSPORT MARKET

208.   The study by Barnes on the effects of partial deregulation of the UK domestic market over the period 1976-1986 showed the following results.   The continuing regulation by the Civil Aviation Authority of route licensing means that for the majority of routes an airline that is performing reasonably well will be protected from the threat of substitution.   For routes that may sustain two (or more) carriers limited forms of price competition may be possible under the terms of the regulations.   However, the number of routes that can sustain two (or more) airlines is limited, and is further constrained by congestion problems at London Heathrow (and possibly Gatwick).

209.   The major effect on prices that deregulation seems to have bought about is a one-off (relative) reduction in the economy price at the time of entry of a new carrier.   However, subsequent price increases have tended to bring fares back to their old level.   Longer term price competition seems to be confined to discount fares.

210.   The market in discount fares has changed considerably over the last 10 years.   There is some evidence to suggest that some of the impetus for the development of these fares has come from competition between airlines.

211.   The majority of the growth of the domestic market has come from expansion in the discount market.   The price of full price tickets has increased faster than the retail price index, while the price of the cheapest discount tickets has tended to reduce relative to full price tickets.   As the number of types of discount tickets available has increased the actual price paid by passengers will have tended to decrease (relative to full price tickets) even faster.

212.   British Airways' dominance of the domestic market has been considerably reduced: in the first instance, by the withdrawal of British Airways from some domestic routes and, more recently, by the reduction of BA's market share on competitive routes.

213.   At least in some areas British Airways' costs are still increasing faster than other domestic airlines and have, in general, been higher to begin with.   However, without data on the costs of BA's domestic operations it is impossible to say whether, overall, BA is more or less competitive than the other airlines or whether it is getting more or less competitive.

214.   The partial relaxation of entry onto existing routes in the early 80's seems to have expanded airline output by increasing traffic on existing routes.   When route entry was confined to opening up new routes, expansion of output seems to have been channelled in this direction.   This would suggest that competition on a single route, even when tightly constrained, tends to increase total output.

215.   Overall, partial competition does not seem to have led to significant reductions in load factors, although there is some evidence that competition

leads to a faster increase in frequency of service, (which must be partially balanced by a reduction in the size of plane used). However, without detailed data on load factors for individual routes it is impossible to check how far this is true outside of the domestic trunk routes.

216.   Overall, partial deregulation seems to have been a success. However, the main impetus to improvement seems to come from the actual entry of a new airline on a route. The number of routes left where this can take place in the near future is limited. Therefore, there must be some doubt about gaining further benefit unless the rules on airline substitution are changed. In addition, the continued dominance of British Airways in a market where its relative competitiveness is unknown where its ability to cross-subsidise is considerable and where it is only lightly constrained from meeting any price competition, must cast some doubt on the future willingness of smaller airlines to compete on price even if this is a reflection of a genuine cost advantage.

D. EFFECT OF THE BILATERAL AGREEMENT BETWEEN THE NETHERLANDS AND THE UNITED KINGDOM

217.   In June 1984, a new bilateral agreement came into effect between the Netherlands and the United Kingdom, which has had an interesting effect on the growth of traffic between the two countries. Table 2 shows the growth during the period 1980-1986.

218.   United Kingdom-Netherlands appeared as an average route in terms of scheduled traffic between 1980 and 1983. As would be expected the non-scheduled traffic growth did not greatly affect UK-Netherlands traffic so total traffic growth was much lower than the UK-EEC average. Since 1983 UK-Netherlands scheduled traffic has grown slightly faster than the UK-EEC scheduled traffic, and kept pace with the air traffic average. Clearly other influences could have an impact on differences in traffic growth patterns (especially shifts between scheduled and charter mode) but it seems quite likely that the change in the Air Service Agreement (ASA) 1984 has been responsible for at least some of the increase in traffic. In comparison with UK-France, where there has not been any significant liberalisation of the ASA, the UK-Netherlands route has grown considerably faster since 1983, after a worse performance before that date. Again, other special factors may be involved but much of the change after 1983 may result from the differences in the respective ASAs from that time. If the differences in growth between UK-Netherlands and UK-France are the result of the differences in the ASAs, this suggests that these might be an increased growth rate of between 3 and 5 per cent per annum as a result of liberalising the ASA.

TABLE 2

Traffic growth on the United Kingdom–Netherlands and United Kingdom–France routes, 1980-86

Percent change

	U.K.-Netherlands		U.K.-France		U.K.-EEC	
	Sched.	All	Sched.	All	Sched.	All
1980/1981	– 5.0	– 4.7	– 0.6	1.1	– 3.0	1.9
1981/1982	1.0	1.7	0.0	2.8	– 2.5	6.3
1982/1983	– 1.3	– 1.9	– 1.0	2.6	0.3	4.0
1983/1984	11.6	11.4	7.5	8.0	10.6	11.6
1984/1985	11.0	10.6	6.6	5.6	9.8	– 0.3
1985/1986	4.7	3.8	– 2.9	– 1.8	3.4	14.4
1980/1983	– 5.4	– 5.0	– 1.7	6.7	– 5.2	12.7
1983/1986	29.4	27.8	11.2	12.0	26.2	27.3

Source: CAA annual statistics

Fares

219.   Under the proposed equivalent EC and ECAC flexibility-zone schemes, the lowest discount allowable in the restrictive deep-discount zone would be equal to 45 per cent of the normal economy fare. To see whether this represents a reasonable lower bound for promotional fares, one needs only to look at the present range of tariffs offered on intra-European routes. In 1984, an IATA study (12) showed that out of a sample of 156 intra-European routes, in not a single one was the lowest discount available more than 50 per cent of the normal economy fare on the route, while in 24 cases - one route out of six - it was less than 30 per cent of it. Existing discounts would not be prohibited under a flexibility-zone system, as most proposals have a preservation clause for existing deep discounts. But it is clear that none of these schemes makes room for revolutionary promotional fares, especially since restrictive conditions on discount tickets are also specified in most proposals. It is also very important, as US experience shows, that deregulation brings a decline in fares effectively paid by travellers, not through a decline in nominal fares, but through a shift of the traffic mix away from normal fares and towards discount fares. Such a process of substitution can only be induced by innovation, on the part of airlines, in the packages they offer.

TABLE 3

London–Amsterdam, Round-trip fares, in UK (£)

	Dec. 1983	Dec. 1985	Dec. 1986
BA/KLM			
Economy (Club Class)	148	162	170
Eurobudget unrestricted	126	138	146
" restricted	105	115	116
PEX	99	109	114
Super PEX	88	91	96
Late booking	–	55	59
BCal			
Economy (Club Class)	´148	162	170
Time flyer Gold	148 (1)	109	116
Time flyer Blue	–	89	106
Time flyer White	98 (1)	69	90
British Midland (Heathrow)			
Standard	–	–	138
Day return	–	–	119
Excursion	–	–	69
Late booking	–	–	39
Transavia (Gatwick)			
Business class	–	–	170
Economy	–	–	140
Promotional (unrestricted until 31/12/86)	–	–	73

Note (1)   In 1983, BCal offered a peak/off peak system called Miniprix.

Source: UK CAA

61

220.   Liberal bilaterals, on the other hand, seem to have a significant
effect on fares.   Tariffs for the London-Amsterdam route are shown in table 3;
they reveal a process which, by now, seems to be fairly predictable: an
increase in nominal fares, particularly in the upper part of the available
range, and a simultaneous multiplication of discount fares.   While the lowest
available promotional fare was, before liberalisation, 59 per cent of Economy
(Club Class) or 70 per cent of unrestricted Eurobudget, it is now 23 per cent
of Economy Club or 27 per cent of Eurobudget.   The change is considerable and
brings us way below the floor of the proposed deep-discount zone.
Furthermore, new concepts of tickets have appeared which show that airlines do
innovate when free, and that restrictive ticket conditions should not be
frozen by multilateral Government negotiations.   Traffic mix data are not
released by airlines; but the latter complain of lower yields on the
London-Amsterdam route, which is precisely the sign of a traffic-mix shift
towards discount tickets.

E.   POSSIBLE EFFECTS OF DEREGULATION IN OTHER REGIONS

1. Structure

221.   Empirical work, especially in the United States, tends to show that a
perfectly contestable market is unlikely to emerge from deregulation.   The
more likely outcome is an oligopolistic structure, with the incumbent airlines
seeking to hold their market share even in the face of new low-cost entry.
However, even if the resulting structure is not perfect, it is likely that the
advantages to passengers outweigh the disadvantages resulting from structural
imperfections when compared with the imperfections inherent in the highly
regulated structures common outside the United States.

222.   The departure from perfect competition in a deregulated industry occurs
for a number of different reasons resulting from the economic characteristics
of airline and airport operation.   The primary result, in Europe, of removing
economic barriers to entry would be to restructure the industry on economic,
rather than nationalistic, lines.   Hub and spoke systems are already well
developed in Europe, but based on domestic feeder services into international
hub airports.   Deregulation could be expected to produce more international
feeder spokes into foreign hub airports, although it should be noted that in
Europe there is probably less scope for hubbing, given the higher proportion
of short journeys, peak-hour congestion at many airports and local resistance
to the expansion or construction of airports.

223.   The nature of European hubs could also be expected to change as their
operation came to reflect underlying economic rather than regulatory factors.
Most importantly, airlines may seek to co-ordinate their route structures into
a centralised hub.   The advantage of this system is that by combining
passengers bound for various destinations, airlines can utilise larger, low
cost aircraft.   These economies, unrecognised at the outset of deregulation in
the United States, will lead to larger size carriers servicing passengers
through a single airport.   Of course, dense routes are still likely to attract
nonstop service outside of the airlines' hub systems.

224.   Subsequently, carriers are likely to seek new hubs at underutilised
airports.   This search for new hubs will occur for two reasons.   First, there
will eventually be diseconomies at any single hub.   Second, business

travellers are known to be attracted to carriers which have frequent services at regular intervals throughout the day. For a business traveller who needs to fly across a hub (i.e. from the end point of one hub spoke to the end point of another spoke) a carrier can only provide a limited number of connections. A second hub would give the carrier a new source of local passengers (those flying only to and from the hub). These passengers, when combined with the beyond passengers, create sufficient traffic for an airline to provide more services using large scale aircraft. An increased number of connections will result.

225. The emergence of hubs will have a predictable effect on the fare structure. The hub system makes service on any flight a joint product, serving local passengers and beyond passengers, business travellers and leisure travellers. In order to capture the maximum revenues for the various market segments carriers will have to inaugurate an extensive price menu. For example, time-sensitive business travellers would be able to reserve seats at any time at higher prices than leisure travellers, who would be limited to a fixed number of seats but at lower prices. Such carriers will have more success than a carrier like People Express, which was unable to capture the available rents from the various market segments that make up the joint product because of its single fare policy.

226. So far, we have seen that in a deregulated environment carriers will seek to expand their existing hubs as well as extend their geographic coverage into other hubs. This restructuring will be accompanied by a complex fare system designed to capture maximum revenues. The need to inform passengers of this array of complex price/service options available and to market them will require extensive computer capabilities and advertising expenses. In particular, airlines will want to have their computerised reservation system (CRS) in place at travel agents' locations located at their hub. CRS provides an airline with the capability necessary to maximize revenue through fare adjustments. Carriers without this capability may seek partnerships with those who do.

227. There is a possible cost to integration into information services. To the extent that they can bias the information on the CRS in their favour or that the technical capabilities of the system favour the airlines owning the CRS, a carrier will have an advantage over its direct competitors. A competitor would also have to pay for access to the system, giving the carrier who has a large share of travel agent locations for its CRS market power over its competitors in air travel markets. Bias and monopoly access fees, if left unchecked, could lead to serious distortions in consumer choice, and high social costs. Policy makers should be forewarned that these activities could threaten new airlines, and should consider some form of CRS oversight. It is highly unlikely that the market will eliminate the problems, especially because of the difficulty a new carrier would have in developing a CRS competitive with existing systems.

228. As a further possibility, firms may seek to invest in their reputations. Whereas, before deregulation a traveller may have had only one or two carriers to choose from, after deregulation the traveller may have more options especially if all entry restrictions are lifted. Carriers will attempt to differentiate their product to generate brand loyalty from its customers. Two related strategies that airlines will have at their disposal are the extension of on-line services and frequent flyer programmes. By

establishing multiple hubs and by entering into scheduling agreements with smaller feeder airlines a carrier can assure any of its passengers that the airline will always fulfill their needs, whether vacation or business, to any destination by just using one airline. Thus, there are apparent marketing economies to carriers with a wide range of routes (13). Frequent flyer programmes generate loyalty as well by creating award systems that give passengers the incentive to fly with one airline.

229. It is evident then that airlines can achieve substantial economies by expanding toward multiple hubs, acquiring access to information services, and by acquiring new and varied routes. The size of most carriers will tend to be larger than those predicted by the competitive model. Whether carriers will achieve this size through merger or internal expansion is an open question. In the United States, after a period of new entry, consolidation seems to have become the mode for expansion. In all situations, however, competition policy should play the role of balancing the need for firms to achieve efficient size against the possible anticompetitive effects from increased concentration.

2. Performance

230. The many changes expected from complete deregulation should have a beneficial impact on consumers. As already mentioned, there will be a large array of available fares. It is safe to assume that the leisure traveller will pay lower fares than under a regulated regime. The study by Moore (14), confirms an overall reduction in average fare paid in the US market, though is should be noted that charter flights provided insignificant competition in the US prior to deregulation. Even under partial deregulation fares may be lower, too. In the example of London-Amsterdam a discount fare of £90 compares favourably with a regular fare of £170 round trip (15). However it should not be expected that all European fares would fall so dramatically in the wake of liberalisation since non-scheduled services and intermodal competition have exercised some influence on such fares.

231. Fares cannot be treated separately from the level of service. Hub systems lead to increased service from small cities that might not otherwise receive service without subsidy. Also, passage from one destination to another is made easier through on-line services. Deregulation will thus have the effect of lowering fares, increasing service frequency, and increasing availability, even with a smaller number of large scale firms.

232. Even though incumbent carriers are not likely to disappear after deregulation, there will still be a great incentive to reduce costs in the face of new entry. Cost reductions can be achieved by rationalising route systems, and by shedding oversized aircraft purchased under a regulatory system in which prices were set above costs. Much of the cost reductions achieved after deregulation, however, appear to come at the expense of labour inputs. New carriers will have lower labour costs, forcing incumbents to negotiate new wage contracts.

233. The effects on labour are well documented in the US experience. These effects have occurred even under less radical forms of deregulation. For example, TWA cut its staff by 27.5 per cent between 1979 and 1982, while British Airways reduced staff by one-third by 1983. In many cases the remaining employees were asked to accept wage freezes. Yet, even with

carrier-specific lay offs, the output from new airlines and expansion of other existing airlines, should dictate an increase in the level of total employment in the industry.

234. Another aspect of performance concerns the overall quality of service. In particular, the questions of flight delay and airport overcrowding arise because while airline output will increase rapidly, airport capacity will remain fixed in the short run. The search for economies in their route systems will force carriers to expand to many new cities out of a single hub airport. Also, competition among carriers will be manifested in the form of schedule competition. Carriers will schedule flights at those times which are convenient for their high revenue passengers. With fixed facilities, overcrowding may result, making restrictions on access necessary.

Airport Access

235. Unlike air transport routes, where restrictions on entry are almost entirely artificial, constraints on access to airports are usually a reflection of real physical limitations. The arguments for deregulation of access to routes do not necessarily apply to access to airports. Indeed, as airport capacity constraints are real, regulation may be necessary to ensure that monopoly exploitation of airport facilities does not take place. In general, current practice at airports gives encumbent airlines perpetual monopoly rights to airport slots. This clearly puts new entrant airlines at a disadvantage and can be a significant barrier to entry. Market solutions to this problem have been both suggested and tried with reasonable success in the United States. This may result in allocative efficiency, but in highly regulated air transport markets its major effect may be to raise the cost base of the airline industry, hence raise the prices faced by passengers. If prices are not to rise unnecessarily some other kind of allocation mechanism may be necessary. As yet these issues have not been addressed in great detail but in many instances the possibility of increased market entry can only be ensured if the airport access problem is solved.

Flight Delays and Airport congestion

236. Growing concern over flight delays in the US has recently prompted action by the Department of Transportation (DOT). Many flight delays are the result of airline competition stimulated by deregulation and have resulted in a bunching of schedules at peak hours. In August 1987, DOT and six major airlines signed agreements to reduce delays at four major airports. In addition, the DOT announced new rules for required data that certain air carriers must submit to the DOT so that information on air carriers' quality of service can be made available to consumers, including data on the on-time performance of all flights from the 27 largest US airports.

Safety

237. Another issue of concern when analysing airline deregulation is the question of safety. In the United States, the Federal Aviation Administration continues to regulate air safety. Many fear, however, that competition among airlines, and the consequent incentive to reduce costs, might cause the

carriers to compromise safety to gain a competitive advantage. Yet accident rates continue to decline. The number of fatal accidents in US civil aviation in 1986 was 1.06 for each 100 000 hours flown, a decrease from 1.2 in 1985 (16). Kanafani and Keeler (17) looked at the question of safety and deregulation. They studied a panel of jet-operating airlines, including new entrants since deregulation and large, established carriers in existence over several decades. Overall, the results indicate that the new carriers studied have safety records just as strong as those of the established carriers. By some measures incumbents are safer than new entrants, and by other measures the reverse is true. However, in all cases, the differences between the two carrier groups are statistically insignificant. In his report for the European Parliament's Committee on Transport (18), Mr Georgios Anastassopoulos says that even when the aviation accidents and fatalities of the "black year" 1985 are included, commercial aviation in the US appears markedly safer in the seven years after deregulation (1979-85) as compared to the five years prior to deregulation (1974-78). The accident and fatality rates have dropped significantly for each segment of commercial aviation for which data are available. Whether the air control system is adequate to maintain the record and to handle the increased traffic resulting from deregulation remains an open question with safety experts. However, the appropriate response to defects related to safety regulation or air traffic control is to rectify the problems directly (i.e. increasing safety regulation or air traffic control capabilities). Trying to solve these problems by the economic regulation of airlines is unlikely to be either efficient or effective.

CHAPTER V

MAIN COMPETITION POLICY ISSUES

238.   In most Member countries competition laws and policies apply to the air transport sector, at least to a limited extent, subject to overriding forms of national and international regulation. As deregulation proceeds, competition policy will become increasingly important to this sector and serve as a crucial instrument in allowing the functioning of market forces in a totally or partially deregulated environment. Moreover, competition policy approaches can in themselves constitute a dynamic factor for change as they challenge some of the underlying concepts of regulation.

239.   In order for competition to function effectively in the air transport industry, as in any other sector, it is essential that entry to the sector be liberalised. More liberal market entry allows new or innovative carriers to provide the competitive impetus which can result in a wider choice of fares and improved services for the consumer. Equally significant is the willingness of States to provide more fifth freedom rights for foreign carriers. Fifth freedom rights are particularly important to carriers which cannot rely on a large domestic market and depend heavily on international air transport markets.

240.   Many of the existing exemptions to competition laws result from the fact that existing national regulation of the industry explicitly restricts competition. For example, rules governing market entry, price approval mechanisms and the restrictive granting of traffic and route licences in both domestic and international markets all fall into this category. If competition is to increase these regulations need to be reappraised.

241.   This is not to say that competition laws and policies are a panacea for resolving all problems which arise. In some countries transition towards a more competitive market structure will be a gradual one and governments may wish to retain residual authority to intervene in instances of severe market failure. Taking into account the specific characteristics of the industry and a perceived need to smooth the adjustment process, governments may also choose to modulate the enforcement of competition laws in air transport by exemptions targeted to specific practices or situations. In these cases, it is important that such exemptions are granted on a temporary basis and that their justification is regularly reviewed.

242.   A number of important competition issues arising in air transport are discussed in the chapter as follows:

    -- Inter-airline rate-fixing agreements;

-- The competition issues related to airline capacity arrangements and pooling agreements;

-- Policies relating to airline mergers and joint ventures;

-- Access to airports and slot allocation;

-- Competition issues arising from computer reservation systems;

-- Action against abuses of dominant positions or attempts towards monopolisation;

-- Promotion of international competition in air transport services.

This analysis is intended to set forth a number of general criteria which are offered for the consideration of Member countries when applying or extending their competition laws and policies to passenger air transport.

A. INTER-AIRLINE RATE-FIXING AGREEMENTS

243.   Following the establishment of ICAO at the end of the Second World War, IATA was given its role to submit tariff recommendations to governments. At the time, it was thought that airlines had expertise in the tariff field which governments did not and that there was a need for a coherent multilateral fares and rates structure, which would assure that interlineability would be maintained.

244.   In recent years, however, governments have begun to re-think the desirability of international rate-fixing through IATA, even though governments retain the power to approve or disapprove the rates submitted. In 1979 the US Government threatened to withdraw antitrust exemption from carriers, foreign or domestic, participating in IATA rate-fixing activities. For foreign carriers, this was only withheld when European carriers agreed to accept "zones of flexibility" on North Atlantic fares. Australia too, has withdrawn its interim approval of IATA rate-fixing activities. Moreover, recent liberal bilateral agreements between the United Kingdom and several European countries allow relatively free pricing by carriers in the country of origin, with no reference to IATA rate-making.

245.   For the future, multilateral rate-fixing may assume a diminishing role as bilateral or multilateral agreements allow more flexibility of pricing by individual carriers. The December 14, 1987 agreement among EC countries as well as a similar agreement reached within ECAC, for example, also allows "zones of flexibility" on intra-European routes, with carriers not being required to have certain "discount" or "deep discount" fares approved by governments nor, in some instances, by other carriers operating on the routes. As another consequence, the EC competition rules have also become directly applicable to restrictive business practices by airlines. IATA, too, has reduced its own role in rate-fixing, which now accounts for only around 20 per cent of the organisation's activities. Participation of IATA carriers in rate-fixing activities has been voluntary since 1980.

246. In the light of these developments governments should reappraise existing fare approval mechanisms and exemptions granted for concerted rate-fixing by airlines.

B. COMPETITION ISSUES RELATED TO AIRLINE CAPACITY ARRANGEMENTS AND POOLING AGREEMENTS

247. Capacity arrangements and pooling agreements are nearly always closely linked. General principles of capacity sharing are initially decided by governments in bilateral discussions; pooling arrangements may form part of the airline commercial agreements which translate the bilateral government decisions on capacity and other issues into daily practice. Airlines have tended to supplement the formal agreements with confidential understandings and side agreements which may substantially modify the practices provided for in the published accords.

248. In this report "pooling" has been considered in its broader sense as the principal aspects of commercial agreements which lead to joint or concerted action by airlines, whether or not they involve the sharing of revenues.

249. Following this approach the following types of airline pooling arrangements call for an analysis of their impact on competition:

1. Agreements to suppress competitive services;

2. Joint operations;

3. Royalty agreements;

4. Capacity sharing;

5. Revenue pools;

6. Revenue-cost pools;

7. Agreements to co-operate on computer reservation systems;

8. Code-sharing agreements;

9. Joint scheduling agreements;

10. Technical joint undertakings.

250. Critics of pooling assert that it represents an unwarranted restraint on competition because it reduces the range of market-oriented products. They also insist that it diminishes the pressure on airlines to compete, to reduce costs, and consequently to become more efficient. The advocates of pooling claim it has a number of advantages as well: it is said to provide a necessary incentive for airlines to operate outside of profitable periods, to improve their load factors, and to contribute to a more efficient utilisation of aircraft and airports. For the consumer, the airline co-operation which is a consequence of pooling is said to be an important factor in retaining the advantages of the interline system.

251. To determine whether the efficiencies of pooling outweigh its anticompetitive features it is necessary to look separately at each of the above-mentioned arrangements to judge whether there is a reasonable balance of benefits between airlines and users. It is also worthwhile questioning whether there are alternatives to pooling which could serve the same purpose that pooling was designed to serve. On the basis of this balancing test the various agreements seem to fall under the following broad categories:

-- Agreements which may have strong anticompetitive effects with little redeeming value;

-- Agreements where anticompetitive effects may be offset by certain efficiency gains;

-- Agreements which do not seem to raise significant competition concerns under normal circumstances.

1. AGREEMENTS WHICH MAY HAVE STRONG ANTICOMPETITIVE EFFECTS

i) Agreements to suppress competitive services

252. Among the most anticompetitive concerted actions are those in which two airlines agree to maintain only a certain level of services on a route. One such agreement specified that the two carriers involved agreed to concentrate on scheduled flights and not to let charter traffic take precedence on routes between their two countries (1). It is difficult to discern the consumer benefits in such agreements, though they are undoubtedly helpful to airlines in maintaining high yields.

ii) Joint operations

253. In a joint operation, a single airline may operate on a route or a route system on the basis of a joint cost and revenue sharing agreement with another carrier or simply in a revenue sharing agreement. In some cases, these agreements allocate one route to one airline and a second to another, both routes being operated in the joint interest. In either case, competition is excluded from the route.

254. While certain routes may not have sufficient traffic to support two carriers, a pooling agreement may not be the preferable way to address the problem. There are more than 100 regional carriers in Europe, many of which serve thin routes quite effectively. One answer would be for governments to designate more regional carriers to serve the underdeveloped routes. The E.C. Council decision of 14th December 1987 contains a provision to allow smaller airlines to serve the category 1 airports, and this step should resolve some of the difficulties. In the United States, regional carriers now serve many of the routes abandoned by the majors after deregulation came into force. Though there have been questions raised about the cost and quality of the services, it is nonetheless true that very few small communities or middle-sized cities have lost air service in the United States as the result of deregulated environment.

255.   Moreover, the concept of a "thin route" may well be a fluid one; routes which now appear able to support only one carrier could possibly support two or more if there were a greater range of consumer choice. Except for joint ventures, creating a new competitor to enter certain markets where individual entry by the partners may not have occurred (see discussion of joint ventures) the market allocation and output restricting effects of joint operation agreement do raise serious competition concerns and can rarely be justified by efficiency gains.

iii) Royalty agreements

256.   Royalty agreements are special types of joint operations which involve one carrier paying a royalty to another for the privilege of the first carrier flying a route for which the second also has traffic rights. One such agreement, apparently no longer in force, allowed one national carrier to keep the route between its capital and another country to itself in return for a substantial cash payment. For the same reasons given in the preceding paragraphs, these agreements display significant anticompetitive aspects with little redeeming value from a user perspective.

iv) Capacity sharing

257.   Thus far discussions on capacity sharing especially within Europe, have tended to focus on figures and percentages. But beyond that, the deeper question needs to be addressed, if capacity sharing is at all appropriate, except perhaps for a short transitional period to ease the adjustment process. In the United States, capacity sharing agreements are forbidden, and in bilateral agreements on North Atlantic routes and elsewhere, the Americans have succeeded in negotiating an unrestricted capacity regime. This has had the advantage of producing more consumer choice. However, the question arises as to whether perceived benefits of capacity controls -- more orderly markets, the prevention of domination by stronger carriers -- more than outweigh the disadvantages of restricted market products and lack of sufficient reward for efficient airlines.

258.   First, the inherent difficulties of finding a satisfactory measure of capacity controls should be underlined. Capacity may be measured on the basis of total available seat kilometres (ASKs) the participating airlines will be flying on a single route; it may also be measured by the frequency of flights or the size or type of aircraft involved. It may be divided on an individual-route basis or on a country-pair basis.

259.   If capacity sharing according to ASKs leads up to a division, say 55/45 on the basis of all routes between two countries, airlines are in a position to choose a rigid split on some routes while others could be selectively liberalised. If country A, for example, wanted to preserve its equal share of the ASKs on flights to the capital of country B, it could simply loosen up capacity on two or three less important routes so long as the total country-to-country traffic added up to the required capacity division. This selective easing of capacity restraints has two consequences: it increases the possibility for market manipulation and control and may artificially favour one route over another without reference to market efficiency and demand. On

the other hand, an ease of capacity control on a city-pair basis would be more efficient from a market perspective.

260. It should also be noted that capacity cannot be considered separately from questions of multiple designation and market entry. As restraints in these fields are eased under bilateral agreements, the rationale for airline capacity arrangements will gradually diminish. In the meantime there are alternative means to achieve the necessary spread of services throughout the day or during less busy periods or on less busy routes which is advanced as the main argument in favour of joint planning and co-ordination of capacity by airlines (scheduling arrangements will be discussed separately below). One is to offer special fares at off-peak hours to encourage more passengers to fly on other than early morning or late afternoon flights. One British carrier, British Caledonian did have such a plan; its "Time Flyer" fares offer travellers a choice of several different tariffs depending on the time of day they depart or return.

261. Another alternative is for governments to use powers they already have to designate more carriers on busy routes and, as suggested previously, more regional carriers on thin routes. To allow capacity sharing other than perhaps for a short transitional period would encourage neither of these alternatives and perpetuate a system of market control which allows little experimentation.

v) Revenue pools

262. Revenue transfers are a common feature of commercial agreements; ECAC in 1982 found that 100 per cent of European pools involved a transfer of revenues, either with or without a ceiling on the amount to be transferred (2). A revenue transfer in an agreement fixing capacity, for example, may require one carrier to compensate another for the second carrier's agreement to schedule a flight at a less convenient time. Revenue pools generally set up a mechanism for transfer based on "notional yield", calculated on the previous year's average income. Each participant's notional revenue is arrived at by multiplying the number of passengers by this standard unit.

263. Transfers of revenue based on notional yield tends to disadvantage a carrier offering discount fares at lower levels than the other pool partner. An airline discounting, on average, more than its partner may have to transfer excess revenue it did not earn, since discounting is not weighted to reduce an airline's share in the pool. Since this procedure discourages airlines from offering lower fares, it is one of the most anticompetitive aspects of revenue pools.

vi) Revenue-cost pools

264. Pools which involve the sharing of costs and revenues represent only about 10 per cent of intra-European pool agreements, according to the COMPAS Report. Such pools involve splitting both the risks and the awards and thus institute a severe mechanism of market control in restraint of competition.

2. AGREEMENTS WHERE ANTICOMPETITIVE EFFECTS MAY BE OFFSET BY EFFICIENCY ENHANCING ASPECTS

265.   The following types of agreements appear to have less significant impacts on competition and may contribute to certain efficiencies in the air transport system.

i) Agreements to co-operate on computer reservation systems (CRSs)

266.   As it will be pointed out later, the threat to competition posed by CRSs is greater when these systems are under the control of a single vendor-carrier who may be tempted to bias the CRS displays in favour of its own flights than when several airlines jointly own a system. When groups of carriers combine in a market pool to offer a CRS, this tends to broaden the base of system information and to build in safeguards that no single carrier will be able to slant display criteria its way.

267.   Similar considerations will apply if the operation of the system is carried out by a joint venture in which different airlines participate. However, whether the scheme is qualified as a joint venture or an agreement, it is essential that services of participating carriers are listed on a non-discriminatory basis and that other airlines may have access to the system on equal terms.

ii) Code-sharing agreements

268.   More ambiguous marketing and service agreements are the so-called "code sharing" agreements linking smaller carriers and the majors. In large part, these agreements have resulted from the CRS dispute; priority on computer screens tends to go to direct flights and to online connections, which disadvantage smaller carriers offering feeder services. As a consequence, increasing numbers of both American and European smaller carriers have signed agreements to share the larger carriers' two letter identification code for the purposes of achieving better CRS display placement.

269.   Code-sharing has sometimes resulted in a blurring of identity between the two carriers, smaller carriers losing their independence and operating under the control of the majors. Competitively, this may reduce the number and variety of smaller carriers. At the same time, service to the consumer may improve in many instances, because of the higher standards for equipment and service. At all events, merger control provisions can be employed if anticompetitive effects result from a merger preceded by code-sharing.

270.   The effects on competition and consumer benefits are therefore mixed and each arrangement of that type should, therefore, be evaluated on a case-by-case basis taking into account the advantages of linked services for consumers.

271.   Whatever the decision, however, there is one element of code-sharing which should be the subject of greater transparency: when a passenger is booked on a feeder flight bearing a major's code, he should be clearly advised of the type of service he will be receiving -- whether turboprop or jet -- and

be able to identify the carrier actually offering the service, regardless of the code it bears.

iii) Joint scheduling agreements

272. Joint scheduling agreements are frequently a feature of capacity sharing pools; however, they can also exist on their own, without a capacity sharing component.

273. Following deregulation in the United States, users and carriers experienced serious problems linked to scheduling as airlines bunched their schedules to take advantage of early morning and late afternoon peak demand and delays have become chronic. A limited antitrust exemption has been granted by the US Department of Transport to alleviate these problems, arguing that both airlines and users would benefit from a degree of co-operation among airlines in schedule planning. While there may be some anticompetitive aspects to such planning, these may be offset by a reduction in costs and congestion at airports and in passenger convenience. Joint schedule planning may be useful for peak period travel, with an agreed definition of the hours a peak period should include. However, airline co-operation should not extend to the drawing up of joint schedules for all daily flights or for agreements to share capacity, and carriers should retain full flexibility on schedules for non-peak flights, when the detrimental effects on costs and convenience are likely to be minimal. It should be noted that the United States Department of Justice has raised strong objections to such agreements on the grounds that they raise a very significant danger of anti-competitive collusion among competing carriers. The Department of Justice recommended market solutions to these problems including the selling of slots.

3. AGREEMENTS WHICH UNDER NORMAL CIRCUMSTANCES WOULD NOT RAISE COMPETITIVE CONCERNS

274. Joint undertakings among airlines concerning technical and operational ground handling, refuelling and security services, handling of passengers, mail, freight and baggage at airports and in-flight catering would seem to fall into this category provided that the sharing of these services is arranged on a non-discriminatory basis and that outside carriers are not excluded from essential facilities at airports. It is essential, however, to ensure that such arrangements which are generally efficiency-enhancing do not lead to collusion among participants in other areas of commercial practice.

C. CONTROLS OF AIRLINE MERGERS AND JOINT VENTURES

275. Based on US experience, concern has been expressed with the recent trend towards consolidation and concentration within the air transport industry. While concentration in itself is not a sufficient yardstick for measuring the degree of competition, care should be exercised that, within relevant markets, oligopolistic structures do not lead to collusion.

276. Generally, airline mergers are subject to assessment under the general merger control provisions in Member countries, the general features of which have been summarised in the Committee's 1984 Report on Merger Policies and

Recent Trends in Mergers (*). Within this framework special questions arise as to the appropriate definition of the relevant market for air transport services as well as to the entry barriers into these markets.

277. As an appropriate starting point the analysis of relevant markets should focus on city pairs. Recent studies in the United States have indeed shown a relationship between concentration and higher prices in such markets. The city-pair test becomes particularly important in the case of mergers of airlines with overlapping hub operations as a new competitor seeking to discipline the market power of the combined airline could not successfully enter without a complete hub operation of its own. Given the substantial economies of scale linked to hub-and-spoke systems, competition from non-stop services or connecting flights may not be a full substitute, especially on short-haul routes.

278. Constraints on essential facilities at busy airports may constitute significant barriers to new entry as may the dominance of computer reservation systems by particular airlines. If scarce airport slots for essential flight times are in the hands of merging airlines, the resulting firm may have excessive market power. It is interesting to note in this connection that in the investigation of the British Airways/British Caledonian merger in the United Kingdom by MMC, the proposal by BA to return slots to the Civil Aviation Authority was one of the factors in the MMC's conclusion that the merger should be allowed to proceed.

279. Where, despite these problems, mergers creating the risk of market power are allowed to go ahead in order not to stifle restructuring or efficiency gains, care should be taken that route licences, where they exist, or slots are not automatically transferred through the operation but reallocated by the competent authorities or through appropriate divestiture by the airlines concerned. In certain merger cases divestiture of other essential facilities such as CRSs may also be appropriate.

280. These considerations would also apply to integration of existing services on specific routes by means of joint ventures between actual or potential competitors. On the other hand, the setting up of new operational units by competitors to enter new routes can enhance competition and would normally be allowed to proceed in the absence of anticompetitive spill-over effects or unreasonable ancillary restraints. In this context, account could be taken of, for instance, the interests of carriers located in peripheral geographical areas to improve their competitive position by gaining access to more centrally situated hub-and-spoke systems. Where joint operations do not involve the creation of efficiency-enhancing facilities or a real commitment of productive resources they should be viewed as pooling agreements to be assessed according to the considerations mentioned above. As to the evaluation of the competitive impacts of genuine joint ventures, reference is made to the multi-criteria approach set out in the Committee's 1986 Report on Competition Policy and Joint Ventures (3).

D. ACCESS TO AIRPORTS AND SLOT ALLOCATION

281. With an increase in air traffic following deregulation as it occurred in the United States, access to scarce airport facilities and, in particular, to gates and slots has become a crucial issue for competition and this is an

area where continued monitoring or regulation may be required to prevent unfair or exclusionary practices by incumbent airlines with market power. Whether the procedure for allocating slots is based on market principles or on the "grandfather rights" principle administered by airport scheduling committees, government authorities dealing with competition in air transport should take into account these constraints in cases concerning mergers and dominant positions.

E. COMPETITION ASPECTS OF COMPUTER RESERVATION SYSTEMS

282.   The development and main features of computer reservation systems have been briefly mentioned in earlier chapters of the report and are described in detail in Annex I. The competition issues surrounding these systems can be characterised as follows:

-- With the growing expansion of air transport in OECD countries, choice of fares and services has become more complicated and users have become increasingly dependent on the services of travel agents;

-- Travel agents, in turn, have become more dependent on CRSs to sort out the range of air fares available to their customers and to book car hire, hotels and a variety of other travel services, which, along with their ability to perform back-office functions, have made CRSs indispensable to many travel agents;

-- The impact of CRSs on airline distribution systems has been profound, and the control of distribution exercises considerable market power through information control, which affects the service side of the air transport industry as well;

-- In the United States, three vendor-carriers control the CRSs at more than 80 per cent of the country's travel agents, raising the question of whether an oligopolistic structure in the distribution sector threatens to restrict consumer choice and lead to greater concentration in airline services;

-- The concerns about concentration have been heightened by contentions that CRSs have been biased in favour of vendor-carriers' flights, which slants information available to users and puts at a competitive disadvantage other carriers participating in the systems;

-- There are also antitrust issues related to market dominance: whether the large CRSs are charging travel agents and other carriers excessively for their services and, by virtue of their market power, establishing de facto monopoly pricing; whether the information fed by participating carriers into the systems of vendor-carriers provides the latter with an unfair competitive advantage in planning selective discounting and other marketing strategies; whether long-term CRS contracts with travel agents unduly restrict the agents from seeking out competing systems;

-- For smaller carriers, the issue is whether CRS dominance by trunk carriers and display criteria favouring major trunk line connections has compelled the smaller carriers to code share with the majors and thereby to lose their marketing independence.

283. These issues have raised the question of whether government regulation should be employed to establish the conditions under which competition in distribution systems could more effectively flourish. Internationally, the principal question is whether national laws should be invoked to protect local distribution systems against the perceived threat of unfair competition. The issue could be effectively addressed by the development of an international Code of Conduct on CRSs; already within Europe ECAC is working on a European-wide CRS Code.

284. In general the anticompetitive nature of oligopolistic control of CRSs by vendor-carriers should be measured against its undoubted efficiencies, the vertical integration of carriers and service systems which produce all-purpose travel services for the user.

285. If government regulation is to be imposed, the key question is whether it can be effective in promoting competition or whether it will be counterproductive and merely create a new set of problems and raise competition issues as serious as the ones it was designed to correct. Past government efforts to improve the competitive environment have faced considerable difficulties without being entirely successful. In particular, regulation to ban discriminatory pricing should take care not to induce a single higher price which smaller carriers could not afford and regulation to reduce CRS bias runs the risk of creating new biases. Perhaps the most promising role for government action would be to improve the conditions for market access for new CRSs, particularly through setting shorter limits on the duration of CRS contracts and establishing more equitable formulae for liquidated damage settlements. Even without these government actions, recent developments indicate that competition among CRSs is likely to increase.

286. In the meantime competition laws provide for the necessary means of action to challenge abusive or exclusionary practices of dominant carriers owning CRSs. The remedies applied should be commensurate with the problem identified and should not stifle technological change and innovation in an area of considerable benefit for providers and users of services. Thus divestiture of CRSs should only be envisaged as a means of last resort to deter serious anticompetitive practices of dominant vendor-carriers or in merger cases if the merger would otherwise create unacceptable entry barriers through exclusive control of the systems.

F. ABUSES OF DOMINANT POSITIONS

287. In this context issues of predatory pricing or non-price predation of dominant carriers may arise. These issues will not be treated in detail as they are subject to a separate study in a more general context and there is no reason why the considerations developed in that report should not be applicable to behaviour by airlines (4). This section is, therefore, limited to a few brief remarks referring to particular conditions prevailing in the air transport industry.

288. The airline industry seems to fall within those industries where predatory pricing behaviour cannot be ruled out as a possible strategy as most

carriers operate in multiple markets (city-pairs) with the possibility of cross-subsidisation, if entry is difficult or regulated. Concerning the criteria to be applied to the assessment of alleged predatory strategies, market power, as in other industries, is an essential prerequisite. On the other hand, the specific cost structure of the industry is such that cost-based formulae such as the one developed by Areeda/Turner is difficult to apply at least as the predominant criterion. In particular, pricing at short-term marginal cost, in certain circumstances, may not be objectionable as the cost to the airline of filling an empty seat approaches zero as flight time nears and consumers and the airline are both better off if low-price stand-by tickets are available without regard to the full or variable costs of the flight as a whole. Thus non-cost-based indicators may be of particular importance for assessing predatory behaviour within this industry.

289. As a general rule issues of predatory pricing should be treated with great care so as not to outlaw flexible and highly competitive strategies which are of benefit to users. In fact issues of non-price predation may be more prevalent, some of which, like abuses of CRSs or airport slots, have already been mentioned. Other practices such as discriminatory conditions in the use of ground and maintenance facilities which are under the exclusive control of an airline or airports or the proliferation of frequent flyer bonus systems granted by large diversified airlines may also give rise to concerns.

G. INTERNATIONAL COMPETITION

290. Two issues arise in this context. The first relates to the potential for conflicting application of national competition laws to international air transport, including ancillary services such as CRSs. In this area, as in other areas of competition law enforcement, co-operation on the basis of the 1986 Council Recommendation is essential if obstacles to international transactions are to be avoided.

291. The second question is the perspective for international liberalisation of air transport services. As pointed out earlier in the report, these services are governed by a network of bilateral agreements regulating air traffic and limiting competition. As in the case for other services, air transport is outside the framework of the present GATT system and work in the OECD on a conceptual framework on trade in services in relation to the Uruguay Round has not yet been extended to that sector. It should be stressed, however, that the OECD Code of Liberalisation of Current Invisible Transactions applies to air transport and on-going work to update this Code may well include further efforts toward liberalisation in this area.

292. There is a close relationship between deregulation and liberalisation: where access to national markets is severely regulated or controlled by national monopolies, where routes are operated by designated carriers on an exclusive basis or under capacity-sharing agreements there is not much scope for extending international competition.

293. On the other hand, deregulation in itself does not bring about international liberalisation. In those countries that have partially or totally deregulated their domestic market, free entry does not typically extend to foreign nationals. Foreign airlines are generally precluded from carrying purely domestic traffic (cabotage) and investment by foreign

nationals or foreign-controlled enterprises in national airlines remains severely restricted. Nevertheless, as deregulation in domestic markets increases the efficiency and competitiveness of carriers under the force of competition, it will provide a powerful incentive for those carriers to expand their services abroad and thus create pressures toward international liberalisation. Progress in this field ultimately depends on the willingness of governments to accept a higher degree of international competition and a certain multinationalisation of corporate structures in air transport, away from a strict policy of protecting national flag carriers.

NOTES AND REFERENCES

CHAPTER I

1. Rigas Doganis: Flying Off Course: the Economics of International Airlines, George Allen and Unwin 1985, pp. 9-10, based on ICAO data.

2. The Economic Situation of Air Transport, Review and Outlook 1986, ICAO Circular 200-AT/78, 1986, p. 19.

3. Peter Movell, Forecasts for the Intra-European Market to 1990, E.I.O. Travel and Tourism Analyst, March 1986, p. 34.

4. Stephen Wheatcroft and Geoffrey Lipman; Air transport in a competitive European market, E.I.U., 1986, p. 10.

5. National Consumer Council; Air Transport and the Consumer, H.M.S.O., 1986, p. 14.

6. Rigas Doganis, op.cit., p. 138 et seq.

7. Rigas Doganis, op. cit., p. 17-18.

8. World Air Transport Statistics No. 30, IATA, 1985 p. 23.

9. W.J. Baumol and R.D. Willig, "Contestability: Developments since the Book", mimeo, 1986.

10. See Annex III, p. 148.

11. Gillen, Oum and Tretheway: Canadian Airline Deregulation and Privatization, 1985.

12. D.R. Graham, D.P. Kaplan and D.S. Sibley, "Efficiency and Competition in the Airline Industry", Bell Journal of Economics, Spring 1983.

13. G.D. Call and T.E. Keeler, "Airline Deregulation, Fares, and Market Behavior: Some Empirical Evidence", Analytical Studies in Transport Economics, 1984.

14. S.A. Morrison and C. Winston, "Empirical Implications and Tests of the Contestability Hypothesis", mimeo, 1985.

15. M.A. Williams, A.S. Joskow, R.L. Johnson and G.J. Hurdle, "Explaining and predicting airline yields with non parametric regression trees" Economic letters 24 (1987) 99-105, North-Holland; and G.J. Hurdle, R.L. Johnson, A.S. Joskow, G.J. Werden and M.A. Williams "Concentration, Potential Entry and Performance in the Airline Industry (unpublished).

16.   G. Bittlingmayer, "The Economics of a simple airline network", mimeo, 1985.

17.   J. Pavaux: L'économie du transport aérien : la concurrence impraticable, Paris, Economica, 1984, p. 58.

CHAPTER II

1.   Two other "freedoms" have occasionally been granted, though they are not formally recognised in air services agreements: (i) "sixth freedom" rights, which refers to the situation where an airline in country A uses two sets of third and fourth freedom rights to carry passengers from country B to country C via its hub in country A; and "cabotage rights" which refer to rights of an airline in country A to carry passengers between two points in country B. The latter rights are rarely granted.

2.   There are at present 23,000 bilateral agreements covering scheduled services between 200 countries and involving 16,000 airports. International Herald Tribune, May 3, 1985 article entitled "IATA adjusts its profile to meet new pressures".

3.   The European Civil Aviation Conference, created in 1954, is an intergovernmental organisation composed of twenty two Member States: Austria, Belgium, Cyprus, Denmark, Finland, France, Federal Republic of Germany, Greece, Iceland, Ireland, Italy, Luxembourg, Malta, Netherlands, Norway, Portugal, Spain, Sweden, Switzerland, Turkey, the United Kingdom and Yugoslavia.

4.   Council Directive on accident investigation, OJ No. L 375, 31.12.80, p. 32.

5.   OJ No. L 237, 16.08.83, p. 19.

6.   Official Journal of the European Communities, L 374 of 31st December 1987, pp. 1 to 26.

7.   Report on Competition in Intra-European Air Services (COMPAS), ECAC, Doc. No. 25, Paris, ECAC, 1982.

CHAPTER III

1.   Joined cases 209 to 213/84, Judgment of the European Court of Justice of 30th April 1986 in the "Nouvelles Frontières" case.

2.   OJ, L 374 of 31st December 1987 pp. 1-26.

3. Commission decision of 23rd January 1985, OJ L 46 of 15.2.85 "Olympic Airways".

4. Press Release IP(87)215.

CHAPTER IV

1. See Keeler, J., "Airline Regulation and Market Performance", Bell Journal of Economics, Autumn 1972, pp. 399-424..

2. For a detailed discussion of US and UK experience see the reports by Joskow and Barnes, Annexes II and III.

3. Morrison, S. and Winston, C., The Economic Effects of Airline Deregulation, Washington, D.C., Brookings Institution, 1986, pp. 8-9.

4. The Deregulated Airline Industry: A Review of the Evidence, Bureau of Economics, Federal Trade Commission, January 1988.

5. Moore, T., US Airline Deregulation: Its Effects on Passengers, Capital and Labor, Journal of Law and Economics 29 (1986), p. 8-9.

6. Morrison, S. and Winston C., op. cit., pp. 25-33.

7. Ibid. p. 40.

8. Moore, op. cit., pp. 23-24.

9. Examples are:

   -- Bailey, Graham and Kaplan, Deregulating the Airlines, MIT 1985, chap. 9;

   -- Moore, op. cit., p. 16-23;

   -- Morrison and Winston, op. cit., chap. 5;

   -- Call, G. and Keeler, T.: "Airline Deregulation, Fares and Market Behaviour; Some Empirical Evidence" in Andrew F. Daughety, Ed. Analytical Studies in Transport Economics. London: Cambridge University Press, 1985.

   -- Williams, M., Joskow, A., Johnson, R. and Hurdle, G. "Explaining and Predicting Airline Yields with Non-Parametric Regression Trees," Economics Letters, Vol. 24, pp. 99-108.

   -- Hurdle, G., Johnson, R., Joskow, A., Werden, G. and Williams, M. "Concentration, Potential Entry, and Performance in the Airline Industry," paper presented at the Southern Economics Association meetings, Washington, DC, November 1987.

10.   Call, G. and Keeler, T., op. cit., p. 37.

11.   Moore T, op. cit. pp. 1-29.

12.   I.A.T.A., International air fares in Europe, Geneva, IATA, 1984.

13.   Levine M., "Airline Competition in Deregulated Markets: Theory, Firm, Strategy and Public Policy", Yale Journal on Regulation, Spring 1987, p. 443.

14.   Moore, T., op. cit., pp. 1-29.

15.   See Table 3 on Round-trip fare London-Amsterdam.

16.   "Be careful out there", Time, January 12th, 1987, p. 26.

17.   A. Kanafani and T.E. Keeler (1987), "New Entrants and Safety: Some Statistical Evidence on the Effects of Airline Deregulation", paper presented at Transportation Deregulation and Safety Conference, Northwestern University, June 1987.

18.   Report prepared for the European Parliament's Committee on Transport by M.G. Anastassopoulos, Document PE 1/2.116, August 1987.

CHAPTER FIVE

1.   Susan Carey, "EC Panel Takes Step in Legal Bid to Boost Airline Competition", Wall Street Journal, August 19, 1986.

2.   Report on Competition in Intra-European Air Services, op.cit., p. 41.

3.   Competition Policy and Joint Ventures, OECD, Paris 1986, pp. 94-96.

4.   Predatory Pricing, OECD, (forthcoming).

A N N E X   I

THE IMPACT OF COMPUTER RESERVATION SYSTEMS

ON AIR TRANSPORT COMPETITION

Mr. Ronald KATZ,
Aviation consultant based in the United Kingdom.

BACKGROUND

1.   The issues surrounding computer reservation systems (CRSs) in air transport have arisen as a direct result of deregulation in the US and the incremental liberalisation of air services in Europe and elsewhere. They have developed rapidly and unexpectedly and have raised substantial questions about the impact of CRSs on airline competition.

2.   In the pre-1978 regulated US air transport market, the sale and distribution of airline tickets was handled either by the carriers directly, their interline partners, or an approved travel agent operating on terms collectively developed by the International Air Transport Association (IATA). Before deregulation, America's trunk carriers relied on travel agents for only around 45 per cent of their total sales.

3.   In the years immediately following the onset of deregulation, several developments contributed to a growing reliance of airlines on travel agents and a corresponding growth in the importance of CRSs. These included changes in the route structures of major American trunk carriers, a vast increase in the number and variety of air fares, rapid advances in communications technology, and heavy investments by a few American carriers in automated ticketing systems. The combination of these factors has created a virtual revolution in airline distribution systems in the United States, the implications of which are beginning to be felt in Europe and Asia as air transport policies become increasingly interdependent.

4.   Since 1978, the route structures of American carriers have become largely based on the development of "hub" and "spoke" operations by major operators in high-density markets. By establishing a strong base or hub, these airlines have achieved considerable economies of scale, have benefitted from "feeder" services to their own on-line services, and have positioned themselves to fight off competition from low-cost smaller carriers.

5.   As the trunk carriers expanded beyond their traditional gateways, they found they could no longer rely on their network of sales offices as the principal means of distributing their product. Nor could they keep track of the hundreds of thousands of daily fare changes in a deregulated environment or adjust their marketing strategies accordingly without highly sophisticated equipment.

6.   Airline CRSs were orginally developed by the carriers to automate their passenger seat reservation and ticketing processes. In the early days of deregulation, the CRSs could not communicate with one another, and some still cannot; but as the capacity and potential of the systems became apparent, the intercommunicability of systems was developed and the range of services and data that could be handled were considerably expanded. The most advanced CRSs

can now display the availability of, and make reservations for, hotels, rail and other surface travel facilities and car rental and provide information concerning currency orders, insurance, and other travel-related data. In addition, they maintain airline ticket information and availability on vast numbers of city-pair services. For example, the Pars system owned by Trans World Airlines (TWA) and Northwest Airlines offers worldwide flight availability on more than 141 000 city-pairs and information covering 8 million US and 14 million international fares.

7.   In recent years, the more sophisticated CRSs have also added features to perform back-office accounting functions for travel agents. These additions have given agents more than an all-purpose display hosting other reservation systems and providing complete travel services; they have also provided a more efficient means of managing agents' day-to-day work apart from the reservations process. The consequences of these developments on travel agents' usage of CRS in the United States have been striking: ten years ago, virtually no US travel agent had access to an airline CRS; today approximately 95 per cent of all US travel agents are equipped with one or more (1).

8.   The spread in the use of CRSs by US travel agents has been accompanied by an increasing reliance of users on travel agents to book their tickets, perhaps the result of the number of, and rapid change in, ticket prices that have followed the advent of airline deregulation. Agents now account for more than 70 per cent of all US airline ticket sales, as opposed to around 50 per cent at the time deregulation came into force. With roughly 90 per cent of those sales being issued through automated reservation systems, the power of CRSs as a marketing tool has become apparent (2).

9.   There are basically two types of CRSs in current use: the so-called multi-access systems, such as Travicom in the United Kingdom, which allow agents to access several airlines' databases by a single set of commands and then to choose their preferred features of the databases of the participating airlines; and the single-access systems, which traditionally allowed entry only to the database of the vendor airline. Several single-access systems, such as United's Apollo, American's Sabre, and TWA/Northwest's Pars, also allow other carriers' databases to be accessed directly through the host system.

10.   Several American carriers, notably United and American, have invested heavily in the development of their CRSs. United is reported to have spent $400 million in the initial stages of developing its Apollo CRS; American some $350 million on its Sabre system. The present and chief executive of Covia Corporation, the division of United responsible for Apollo, has estimated the company will spend $1 billion to improve the system, with the bulk of those funds being used to provide improved back-office functions for travel agents (3).

11.   CRS revenues have become an increasingly important factor on the balance sheets of the carriers (called "vendor-carriers") selling their services. American Airlines, for example, earned $140 million in profits from its Sabre CRS in 1986 on a total company turnover of $360 million. Some critics have suggested that these systems have begun to exercise power out of proportion to the vendor carrier's share of the air transport market, a

classic case of "the tail wagging the dog". American's market share in revenue passenger kilometres (RPKs) was only 13.8 per cent of the American market in 1986, yet its Sabre CRS controlled 39.9 per cent of the CRS market the same year (4).

12.   As of May 1987, Sabre and Apollo controlled 68 per cent of the terminals installed at travel agent subscriber locations in the United States. The third largest American CRS, Texas Air's System One, controlled around 15 per cent. Until recently, the American CRS systems had made only modest inroads in Europe. In July 1987, however, Apollo and System One entered into agreements with several European carriers, a development which opened up new competitive questions concerning CRSs internationally. (The details and implications of these agreements are discussed at length in paragraphs 57-63).

13.   European CRSs have not traditionally been highly competitive with one another. They have tended to operate only within the borders of their home countries from a quasi-monopoly position. The stronger European CRSs -- Lufthansa's START, Air France's Esterel, and British Airways' Babs -- have, until recently, also been less versatile than their American counterparts and have offered a more limited range of services to travel agents. Moreover, European air transport has tended to be highly regulated with a more limited and predictable choice of fares. As liberalisation comes to Europe, the role of travel agents and competition among carriers for their services, is likely to expand. The CRS issues that arose in the United States, which have already had a limited impact on Europe, will grow in importance.

COMPETITION ISSUES RAISED BY CRS

14.   For convenience, the competition issues raised by CRS will be divided into two categories -- CRS bias and market domination -- though in reality the issues are interrelated and all centre around the exercise of market power through information control.

A. CRS Bias

15.   Until 1984, the screens of US vendor-carriers were biased in favour of their own flights. CRS bias involved competitor's flights appearing on a later computer screen than the flights of the vendor-carrier even when the competitor's flights were more direct or convenient or were less expensive. The importance of appearing on an early computer screen cannot be overstated: it has been estimated that 90 per cent of a travel agent's CRS bookings are made from the first screen on the video display (5). On certain routes, several screens may be employed, and a carrier's flights appearing on a later screen operate at a distinct competitive disadvantage.

16.   In order to address the anticompetitive aspects of bias, regulations were issued by the US Civil Aeronautics Board (CA) in 1984 to require that CRS primary displays not be based on any factor "directly or indirectly related to carrier identity" but on the basis of consistently applied service criteria.

The regulations also required that vendor-carriers supply on request to any subscribing or participating carriers "the current criteria used in ordering flights for the primary displays and the weight given to each criterion " (6).

17.   In spite of the 1984 regulations, the issue of computer bias in the United States has not been totally resolved. In November 1984, shortly after the regulations were issued, ten American carriers filed suit against United Airlines and American Airlines charging that subtle bias still existed in the Sabre and Apollo displays, enabling the two airlines to earn substantial "incremental revenues". In 1985, United, American, and TWA Airlines, noting that the 1984 regulations only applied to "primary displays", offered travel agents using their system secondary displays with a lock-in feature biased in favour of their own flights. These secondary displays were eliminated after US Congressional leaders wrote to the US Department of Transportation protesting against a violation of the "spirit of the regulations". In June 1986, Delta Airlines, in a suit filed against American Airlines, made the specific charge that American was using "sham schedules" showing a shorter elapsed time (departure to arrival time) on its flights in order to have those flights listed first on its Sabre CRS screen (7).

18.   At present, display criteria call for non-stop flights and one-stop connections to have priority listing on screens; however, this seemingly reasonable listing of preferences has created considerable controversy, particularly for the smaller airlines, as discussed in more detail in paragraphs 37-39.

19.   Moreover, the issue of bias has not been confined to the American market. American carriers and the US government have begun to pursue CRS bias in other countries. Their principal vehicle is the International Air Transportation Fair Competition Practices Act (IAFTCPA) 49 USC Section 1159a-d, which allows US carriers or any agency of the government to file a complaint with the Secretary of Transportation to determine whether a "foreign government or instrumentality, including a foreign air carrier" is engaging in "unjustifiable or unreasonable discriminatory, predatory, or anticompetitive practices against a United States air carrier ... or imposes unjustifiable or unreasonable restrictions on access of a United States air carrier to foreign markets." 49 USC Section 1159(b)1.

20.   The first application of the IATFCPA process to foreign CRSs was initiated against Lufthansa and its participation in the West German START CRS, which is co-owned by the West German national railway and four West German travel agencies. Three American carriers -- Northwest Airlines, TWA, and Pan American -- filed a complaint against Lufthansa and the West German government (Lufthansa's principal shareholder) under IATFCPA, seeking, among other remedies, to have approval of the pending Frankfurt-Houston Lufthansa service held up until the bias against American carriers was eliminated from START's screens.

21.   Though the US-Lufthansa dispute was eventually settled through diplomatic negotiation -- Lufthansa agreed to unbias START's screens against American carriers -- other European governments have also lodged complaints. The United Kingdom, in bilateral negotiations in 1986, expressed concern that the criteria for display which may offer neutrality for American domestic

carriers still contains significant biases against international operators, substantially limiting their access to the US market.

22.   It is clear that bias and other CRS questions have the potential to become divisive issues in international commerce. As with most international competition issues, there are differences of perception and interpretation: in the case of the Lufthansa START system, for example, Lufthansa orginally responded to the American complaint by asserting that American carriers overstated START's importance in the market and that the West German ticketing process was not comparable to the American One. International disputes over CRS bias could lead to further international conflicts, with the possibility, that national competition laws could be invoked internationally in an attempt to resolve the issues involved.

B. Market Domination Issues

i) General concerns

23.   Stated in the simplest terms, the principal market domination issue in the United States is whether, under the anti-monopoly interpretations of US anti-trust laws, two or three giant CRS suppliers will be permitted to dominate and control the primary means of distributing substantial proportions of the entire US industry's product. From a European point of view, the question is whether the movement of giant American CRSs, such as Sabre and Apollo, into Europe will introduce economies of scale against which the Europeans are not prepared to compete and will lead to a loss of commercial control by European carriers over their own product. Moreover, just as American competition laws could be employed against the CRSs of other countries, there is the possibility that European competition rules under the Treaty of Rome could be used in a similar manner against the Americans.

ii) Pricing and profits

24.   Airlines using other vendor-carriers' CRSs are called upon to pay several different charges, depending on the extent to which they use the system.   Among these are "access charges" for participating carriers having agreements with the vendor-carriers for display of the participant's flight schedules, fares, or seat availability, or for the making of reservations or issuance of tickets through the system.   There are also "service enhancement charges" for any product or service over and above the access charges, such as those for car rental, insurance, or back-office accounting assistance.   Travel agents are subject to "booking fees" for each segment of a voyage reserved through a CRS and for any enhanced services they choose to book.

25.   Critics have contended that both access charges and booking fees are too high and they they are creating excess profits for vendor-carriers. Central to this claim has been the contention that vendor-carriers have been earning substantial "incremental revenues" from their CRSs.   Incremental revenues are said to be additional revenues a vendor-carrier earns as the result of an agent using its CRS, i.e., superior access of vendor-carriers to marketing data, continued subtle bias on CRS screens, etc.   Vendor-carriers

contend they are making a fair rate of return based on the huge investments they have made in their systems, and they reject the concept of incremental revenues.

26.   There is broad disagreement about rates of return. At present, American Airlines' Sabre charges travel agents $1.75 for each booking segment and Apollo charges $1.85.   United claims it receives a return of 5 per cent on investment from Apollo.   Consultants for Delta Airlines, which is suing American and Sabre, claim that when incremental revenues are factored in, Sabre is actually earning American a return of 160.5 per cent.   Both sets of figures are currently being examined by the US Department of Transportation.

27.   Prior to the 1984 CAB regulations, US vendor-carriers could and did discriminate among participating carriers in the fees charged for participation in their systems and for system-related services.   After the 1984 regulations outlawed discriminatory charges, United and American each established uniform fees for all users.   One immediate result was an increase in charges -- said to be as much as 264 per cent and 500 per cent for Apollo and Sabre respectively, although some airlines had their fees reduced.   There has been a substantial impact on small carriers, as discussed in paragraphs 37-39.

28.   Critics claim the potential for abuse of CRS pricing in an oligopolistic environment constitutes a major threat to airline competition. They contend that if CRS vendor-carriers extract supracompetitive profits from their systems and raise the costs of their potential rivals, the competitive system will be severely affected.   On airline routes having only slim profit margins, it is said that CRS fees could eat up any profits that might accrue. Moreover, if a few vendor-carriers with market power decided to change their pricing systems, to base them on a percentage of revenue rather than a fee-per-transaction basis, some estimates are that the fees for carriers using one of these larger CRSs could soar as much as 700 per cent.   The Official Airline Guide (OAG) videotext CRS already uses such a pricing system.

iii) Yield management, selective discounting, and access to rivals' confidential information

29.   In a deregulated environment, commercial success can depend on the analysis of profiles of thousands of different flights to determine the proper mix of discount and full fare tickets an airline should sell to maximize yields.   The process of yield analysis, termed "yield management" or "revenue control", is an important feature of a CRS.

30.   In the earlier days of US deregulation, low-cost carriers were the driving force behind the pricing of airline tickets.   Perhaps the primary reason the major carriers have regained control of the pricing process is that their yield management control system have become increasingly sophisticated, allowing them the flexibility to offer a specific number of low-cost fares to compete with a low-cost competitor without reducing the net they receive from peak and business travellers.   Yield control programmes such as American Airlines' DINAMO, can perform a variety of tasks: they can subsidise fare wars in limited markets while maintaining high yields in non-competitive markets;   they can raise the expected load factor or enrich the passenger mix on individual flights.

31.   A CRS is a necessary adjunct to a yield management programme, because it maintains an inventory of the seating availabilities of the carrier seeking to manage its seat allocation. The competition issue is whether CRS vendor-carriers, which have access to the reservations data of airlines participating in their systems, are able to analyze that data in a way that gives them an unfair competitive advantage over rivals who do not have the same quality and availability of data at their disposal. The issue has already been raised in the United States in a suit by Continental Airlines against United and American. Continental claimed that both vendor-carriers were using information supplied by Continental to a CRS to monitor the sales performance of the carrier and to develop competitive strategies to combat some of its marketing efforts. The issues have yet to be resolved, and the implications, both for the confidentiality of business data and the supposedly unfair marketing practices of CRS owners, raise one of the more complicated competitive questions related to CRS ownership.

iv) <u>Barriers to market entry: capital and operating costs</u>

32.   Given the enormous earning potential of CRSs, it would appear that the entry of new systems into the market would be inevitable. Such a development, it is said, would ensure the existence of a competitive market. Critics claim, however, that de facto barriers to market entry are very difficult to overcome. One of these barriers is the heavy costs -- in time, resources, and personnel -- required to start up a system, costs said to be beyond the capabilities of small or moderate-sized carriers. It has already been noted that United plans to spend $1 billion to update and improve its Apollo system; American has reportedly invested a total of more than $3 billion in Sabre.

33.   Apart from capital and operating costs, there are practical difficulties because of a paucity of trained programmers and the long lead time required to catch up with existing CRSs, which are becoming progressively more advanced.

v) <u>Barriers to entry: long-term contracts and liquidated damage clauses</u>

34.   Perhaps the most onerous barriers to entry are said to be the length of vendor-agent contracts and the liquidated damage clauses in a number of them which typically state that an agent breaking a contract before its expiration date must pay the vendor up to 80 per cent of the fees he (the vendor) would have received over the remaining life of the contract.

35.   The US Civil Aeronautics Board, in its 1984 regulations, limited the life of subscriber contracts with vendors to five years. Some sources point out, however, that vendors have been ingenious enough to evade these restrictions, in some instances by claiming that a new contract should be signed whenever new equipment is delivered to an agency location. Through such tactics, it is said that contracts can be extended for up to 12 or 13 years. Even if they are not extended, the contention is that five years is too long for a contract; in Europe, the tendency has been to shorter contracts, running from 2-3 years.

36.   The combination of lengthy contracts and heavy penalties are said to impede agents from seeking out other CRSs, no matter how competitive they may be. This creates a de facto barrier to market access. On the question of damages, the president of one large US travel agency, Northwestern Business Travel, in Minneapolis, Minnesota, has pointed out that if his twelve offices were to cancel an existing contract with the Apollo CRS, he would have to pay approximately $4 million in liquidated damages. In defence of liquidated damage clauses, the president and chief executive of Covia Corporation, which directs Apollo for United Airlines, has asserted that liquidated damage clauses are justified because his company has made a heavy investment in hardware and software, which does not begin to show a profit until the fifth year of the contract (8).

vi) The special problem of smaller carriers

37.   Perhaps no group of American carriers has been more concerned by questions of CRS dominance than the smaller carriers. As noted previously, the 1984 CAB regulations required that vendor-carriers charge non-discriminatory fees to all carriers participating in their systems. Before that time, smaller carriers had generally enjoyed free access to the screens. When the regulations went into effect, vendor-carriers began charging the small carriers the same fees as they charged the majors.

38.   High fees and CRS listings had created pressures to enter into code-sharing agreements with major carriers. Because the 1984 regulations led to the listing of non-stop flights and one-stop connections at the top of the CRS displays, small carriers often found it necessary to be affiliated with a major's two-letter code, which would help to place them at the beginning of the list. Code-sharing may be one of the steps towards a takeover; since the high point of deregulation, the numbers of American smaller carriers have been decreasing at the rate of about 10 per cent a year; of the 254 airlines at the height of deregulation, only 179 remained at the beginning of August 1986 (9). Many of these carriers have been bought out by the majors. Most small airline executives contend that CRS dominance by a few vendor-carriers has been a significant factor in their decision to affiliate with a larger carrier (10).

39.   In Europe, too, small carriers have expressed concern about CRS bias and dominance issues. A survey currently in progress by the Economist Intelligence Unit (11) reveals that 50 per cent of the European small carriers surveyed list CRS problems as one of the three major factors limiting the growth of Europe's regional airlines. The issue, in both Europe and the United States, is whether the efficiencies gained from code-sharing offset the loss of independence of the smaller carriers. For passengers, a closer relationship between small and large carriers may represent an improvement in that there may well be newer and more modern aircraft used, better connections, and service standards equal to those of the majors.

vii) Pressures to participate

40.   When travel agents are located near the major hubs of vendor-carriers, it is said that there are severe commercial pressures on them to use the CRS provided by these carriers. Moreover, there can be pressure on the other

airlines serving these hubs to participate in the system. In many instances, CRSs provided by vendor-carriers serving the carrier's hub have achieved a quasi-monopoly status: in the Dallas/Fort Worth, Texas area, for example, which is a hub for American Airlines, roughly 88 per cent of the automated travel agencies use American's Sabre system. For new entrant carriers in the Dallas/Fort Worth area, participation in Sabre has been said to be virtually essential (12).

41. Some carriers attempting to operate outside of the dominant US systems have also been subject to marketing pressures. Southwest Airlines tried to operate outside of Sabre CRS until American Airlines prohibited Sabre travel agents from turning out Southwest's tickets on their machines. Shortly thereafter, Southwest agreed to sign a Sabre participation agreement (13).

42. Other pressures have been applied in the form of cash inducements urging agents to sign on with certain CRSs. A former vice-president of Northwest Airlines, William Kutzky, told a US Senate subcommittee of one major agent being offered a $500 000 inducement to switch to another system as well as recompense for any penalties for breaking the contract with the original system provider (14). While such inducements can be read as a by-product of open competition, there may be some question as to whether the smaller CRSs can afford to match the economic favours granted by their more capital-intensive rivals.

viii) CRS and the consumer

43. Though most discussion of CRS focuses on the impact of the systems on carriers and travel agents, consumer spokesmen point out that there are implications for users as well. As users have become more dependent on travel agents and agents upon CRSs, the possibilities for manipulation have increased, user spokesmen say. One American carrier, for example, offered agents a special one dollar bonus for every booking on its airline which was switched from another carrier. "Was it the agent's role to act as the user's travel planner or the agent's distributor", one consumer representative asked. He continued: "How can the passenger ensure that his itinerary meets his needs best and doesn't simply have him hubbing and spoking as the software dictates and the incentives encourage?" (15). Some users, while recognising that the rule of caveat emptor applies in a free market, have urged more transparency in CRS services so that a knowledgeable traveller can obtain information from his travel agent about what carrier is hosting his system and what series of priorities it displays.

A. General questions about the appropriateness of regulation in the U.S. context

44.   In the United States, government officials have been concerned that attempts to regulate CRSs could undermine the deregulated air transport system. The theory has been expressed that a free market distribution system will eventually sort out the competitive distortions which may temporarily exist. The point is also made that companies, such as United and American Airlines, which had the foresight and initiative to invest billions of dollars in their CRSs, should be entitled to reap the rewards of their endeavours.

45.   Ranged against these arguments have been those of critics contending that regulation is required because the financial and technological power of existing CRSs makes it unlikely that the market mechanism can function effectively. In this respect, the discussion about CRS regulation mirrors the other discussion taking place concerning the correct government approach to mergers in the airline industry. In that instance, the contention of critics has been that antitrust laws should have been used more aggressively to prevent oligopolistic domination of the market by five or six major carriers. On both issues, there are philosophical and practical questions to consider. This paper will focus more specifically on the practical, namely whether government intervention would be useful in ameliorating the difficulties of the present system, and, if so, what form that intervention should take.

B. Specific regulatory remedies: the United States

Divestiture

46.   Divesting airlines of their CRS systems and diverting these systems to separate and independent companies has been advocated by some observers, including former US CAB Chairman Alfred Kahn as the only truly effective means of maintaining CRS neutrality and ensuring a smoothly functioning market. The point has been made by these observers that CRS bias is subtle and hard to control and that divestiture would eliminate a CRS' profit-making relationship to a carrier and remove the incentive for that carrier to selectively disadvantage other carriers in CRS displays. Moreover, it is claimed that divestiture would eliminate the ability of carriers to use their ownership of CRSs to impede entry and competition in both the CRS market and in the airline passenger market.

47.   Yet divestiture is a severe remedy which also has certain disadvantages. The vertical integration of carriers into the CRS market achieves certain efficiencies which could be lost as a result of divestiture. Moreover, divestiture would be a time-consuming process and shifting CRSs to independent entities would not necessarily ensure that the abuses of the present system would be resolved, since carriers could still form close links with new CRS managing units. Finally, the CRS distribution system is still relatively young, having reached its present stage of development only in the last ten years.

C. Reducing bias

48.   As noted in paragraphs 37-39, government attempts to reduce CRS bias have had unintended consequences, one of which was to speed the consolidation of smaller airlines with the majors. Bias remains one of the most difficult issues to resolve and perhaps the most resistant to government regulation. Unbiasing the system at one point will inevitably create bias at another. Moreover, the pace of technological change in the industry is frenetic, and attempts by governments to monitor change and impose anti-bias rules accordingly would likely prove ineffective. For these reasons, broad anti-bias rules outlawing the most blatant instances of bias -- such as those listing flights of the vendor-carrier before all other flights or relegating rival carriers to the second screen -- may well be the most practicable course for governments to follow. More specific government-imposed rules, such as those requiring that flights be listed in the order of "elapsed time" (departure to arrival time) or with priority on direct connections rather than interline flights, inevitably create distortions, and governments are poorly placed to decide which of the distortions are beneficial for airlines and users. Rules against the most blatant bias accompanied by the requirement for transparency by carriers in defining the criteria they use in screen listings may well constitute the limit to which governments should go in trying to create a neutral listing system.

D. Price controls and excess profits

49.   As in the case of bias, government attempts to enter into the details of pricing policy could turn out to be counterproductive. As noted earlier, government regulations in 1984 outlawing discriminatory pricing were followed by increases in access charges to participating carriers of up to 500 per cent.

50.   At present, the US Department of Transportation is reviewing highly contradictory evidence submitted by vendor-carriers and some of their competitors. There are several points at issue: one is an accounting question, the determination of how a vendor-carrier allocated CRS costs to its agency functions or to its internal operations. Another is whether so-called "incremental revenues" exist and if they do, how they can be factored into the total rate of return.

51.   Regardless of how these issues are resolved, it would seem both impractical and poor public policy for governments to set or regulate prices charged by vendor-carriers. Regulated prices may appear to be an acceptable short-term solution, but, over time, they create distortions that are frequently more harmful than the injustices they were designed to correct. The answer to charges of excess profits would appear to lie in more competition, which is discussed in the following sections on market access. Moreover, even the limited amount of competition now in place appears to be having some effect: as Texas Air's System One challenges the dominant CRSs Sabre and Apollo, the competition for travel agent clients has become intense, and agents have had some success in negotiating lower automation costs and a range of other concessions from vendor-carriers. Sabre's pre-tax margins are expected to drop from 40 per cent in 1985 to 20 per cent in 1987 (16).

E. Improving market access

52.   It may be that the most fruitful area for targeted government intervention would be in measures to encourage market access for other systems. Even though there are no legal barriers to the entry of new CRSs, there are, as has been noted, a number of de facto barriers that render market access extremely difficult.

53.   In 1984, the government set a five year limit on the duration of CRS contracts with subscriber travel agents. This period could be reduce to, say, 2-3 years, which is the typical length of a CRS contract in Europe. If agents are locked into lengthy contracts, they will have neither the incentive nor the opportunity to investigate competing systems. In addition, the government could stipulate that the contract should not be deemed to be extended or substantially modified by the delivery of new equipment or other materials designed to improve and update the CRS; this would avoid the situation in which vendor-carriers perpetuate existing contracts by adding new features to their systems.

54.   With regard to liquidated damage clauses, the government action could focus on developing some general guidelines for relief rather than trying to write a specific formula into regulation. One option would be to require that any liquidated damage settlement should bear a reasonable relation to the costs the vendor-carrier would be subject to if an agent seeks to exit from the contract before its expiry date. The burden of proof should be on the vendor-carrier to demonstrate what his costs would be, and that would be a matter for a court to decide if negotiation with an agent proved to be unsuccessful.

55.   It should be noted that government actions to encourage market access, while perhaps necessary in the short term, could prove to be unnecessary over time if groups of airlines banded together either to buy out an existing CRS or to develop a new one. Past efforts to do so have often been stymied because carriers could not agree on priorities or because adequate financing could not be found. However, the recent agreement between groups of European carriers and American CRSs to enter into joint ventures with one another, as described in paragraphs 57-63 illustrates that such a solution is not beyond the capabilities of airlines and indeed may signal the shape of developments to come.

56.   Nor should it be assumed that airlines will be the only source of new, competing CRSs. Large capital-intensive credit card firms, newspaper chains, hardware and software manufacturers, have all reportedly considered the possibility of starting up new systems. One or two major CRSs from these sources could introduce an element of competition into the field which could obviate the need for government action other than that to adjust the duration and liquidated damage clauses in present CRS contracts.

F. Other factors mitigating the need for government regulation

i) New European-American co-operation on CRSs

57.   There have been several attempts by European countries and their carriers to counter the competitive threat of American CRSs. Some countries pursued protectionist policies to prevent the American systems from gaining a foothold: in West Germany, for example, the Lufthansa START CRS enjoyed a quasi-monopoly status and other CRSs were effectively barred from entry into the market;   in the United Kingdom, attempts by American CRSs to work through the country's bank settlement plan met with substantial difficulties.

58.   There were also earlier attempts by European carriers to work together, sometimes in co-operation with non-CRS owning American carriers, to establish new systems: an IATA-based plan to establish a neutral industry booking system (NIBS) and, in 1986, a project by the Association of European Airlines (AEA), which spent $500 000 on a study to look into the feasibility of a supra-European CRS for Europe's major carriers.

59.   Neither of these attempts succeeded, and in July 1987, two separate groups of European carriers decided to set up new CRSs in co-operation with two of the major American systems. The first group, called Galileo, as of December 1987 consisted of Austrian Airlines, Alitalia, Aer Lingus, British Airways, Swissair, KLM Royal Dutch Airways, TAP (Portugal) and United Airlines' Covia Corporation, the parent company of the Apollo CRS. Galileo is to buy into Covia and Covia has taken an equity share in the Galileo system, though it will own less than one-third of the new company, which will be organised as a separate corporation and have its own management staff. The agreement stipulates that all flight and scheduling will be presented on an unbiased, independent basis. Limited joint operations are to begin in 1988, and a new IBM computer network to power the system is scheduled to be operational by mid-1989.

60.   The second group, called Amadeus, was formed by Air France, Air Inter, Iberia, Lufthansa, and the Scandinavian Airlines System (SAS). It will purchase a licence for its software from Texas Air's System One CRS, and Amadeus staff will receive training and technical support from the American system;   however, System One and Texas Air will not take equity share in the group. The European members indicated they wished to retain independent control of their own distribution systems.

61.   The marketing advantages of the US/European link-up could be considerable. The US carrrier partners will have access to the European travel agencies and the Europeans to the American ones. The hardware will be located in European countries where labour and fringe benefits are lower.

62.   Though important commercial and competitive questions remain, the new European/US alignment has the potential to defuse the growing trade tensions between the US CRSs and their European counterparts, since each will have a stake in the new systems' success. Moreover, the possibilities for bias will be more limited with a broadly-based system since the checks and balances built into multiple ownership will tend to assure that no single carrier will be able to slant display criteria its way. As more European carriers joint one or the other systems -- Amadeus in September invited eight additional carriers to join -- or decide to band together to form an additional system,

the issue of market dominance, at least in the European context, could tend to be dissipated. The American carriers' willingness to accede to the Europeans' terms on ownership and control indicates that the market dominance of American CRSs, if not overstated, has at least begun to adjust to the realities of a world market.

63.   Another possible competition issue concerning whether the common purchase, development and operation of computer reservation systems would constitute a violation of the competition rules of the Treaty of Rome is currently being addressed by the European Commission, which, on 12th June 1987, in a Draft Council Resolution, proposed that such joint agreements be granted a block exemption provided that air carriers of all EC Member States have access to such systems on equal terms, that participating carriers have their services listed on a non-discriminatory basis, and that any participant may withdraw from the system on giving reasonable notice (17).

ii) Alternative distribution systems

64.   The entire complexion of the CRS issue could be altered substantially over the next ten years or so as alternative methods of distributing airline tickets move into active use. New technologies are already opening up the possibility of more direct selling between airlines and customers, without the intervention of a travel agent. In the United States, direct ticketing machines for a limited number of flights are already in place at several airports and shopping centres. And with the strong growth in home computers and systems like videotext, the consumer could have tariff information and flight schedules displayed in his home and have access to a printer which would print out the ticket and provide him with a boarding pass. The development of "smart cards" with imbedded microchips could activate new public machines.

65.   Along with these changes, a declining reliance on travel agents could be accelerated as individual corporations, banks, and mail order firms set up their own travel services, which could be then linked to the customer's home computer. These changes in the distribution system will be more revolutionary than the changes wrought by airline CRSs and they will present a host of new issues: what will be the impact on travel agents and small airlines? How will airlines compete to capture the large corporations and the home user? The answers to these questions will be as complicated in their way as are the present issues surrounding CRSs.

66.   New CRS entrants and alternative distribution systems will not remove the issues surrounding CRSs, which are likely to remain contentious for the next few years. But eventually, they will alter the terms of the debate. The decisions to be taken in the meantime concerning bias, market dominance, and the proper role of government regulation must take into account that the pace of change in the industry is extremely rapid and that solutions which may seem plausible now could well be outdated in a very short time.

NOTES AND REFERENCES

1.   Ray Grainger, Director Travicom, "Computerised Reservation Systems", Aviation Seminar, London March 26, 1987.

2.   Mark Tran, "Airlines Sue Over Reservations Squeeze", Airline Business, January, 1986, pp. 28-30.

3.   Richard Whitaker, "United We Stand?", Airline Business, July 1987, p. 26.

4.   "Action Now on CRS", Airline Business, March 1987, p. 5.

5.   See US Department of Justice, 1985 Report of the Department of Justice to Congress on the Airline Computer Reservation Industry, December 20th 1985.

6.   See Part 255, 14 CFR Chapter 11, US Civil Aeronautics Board.

7.   See Third-party complaint of Delta Airlines, Inc., Complainant v. American Airlines, Inc., Respondent before the U.S. Department of Transportation under Section 411 of the Federal Aviation Act of 1958, as amended, and for violations of the anti-bias provisions of the CRS rules, June 16, 1986.

8.   "A Shoving Match in the Travel Agency", Business Week, 22nd June 1987, P. 60.

9.   Pat Gaudin, "Commuter Blues", Airline Business, October 1986, pp. 34-39.

10. Op. cit., No. 8.

11. The survey is referred to in an unpublished article by the author, "Europe's Regional Carriers: Regulatory Developments and Commercial Projections", to appear in Travel and Tourism Analyst, December 1987.

12. See speech of US Senator Nancy Kassebaum, "Deregulation and Competition: What is Government's Role Now?" to the Wings Club of New York, March 20, 1985.

13. Ibid.

14. Geoffrey Lipman and Stephen Wheatcroft, Air Transport in a Competitive European Market, the Economist Intelligence Unit, p. 93.

A N N E X   I I

DEREGULATION AND COMPETITION POLICY

THE US EXPERIENCE WITH DEREGULATION IN THE AIR TRANSPORT SECTOR

Dr. A. JOSKOW
Economist
Antitrust Division of the US Department of Justice

-- Part one provides an overview of the regulatory framework of the US airline sector and a discussion of empirical evidence on the effects of deregulation;

-- Part two provides an overview of recent trends in the US air transport sector since 1985.

Part One

DEREGULATION IN THE UNITED STATES AIR TRANSPORT SECTOR
-- INSTITUTIONAL FRAMEWORK AND EMPIRICAL EVIDENCE

I. INTRODUCTION

1.   The purpose of this paper is to summarise the experience of the US airline industry since the elimination of domestic economic regulation in 1978. It is hoped that the paper will stimulate discussion on how deregulation might work in other countries. Use of another geographic area as a form of laboratory experiment to assess policy can be a very useful technique. In the US, for example, it was the study of unregulated, intrastate airlines in Texas and California that provided the necessary laboratory. In most cases the unregulated intrastate fares were considerably lower than those in interstate markets of comparable size and distance. Although the US domestic industry remains in transition, it is hoped that this paper will form a useful framework for further discussion and study.

2.   Part one of the paper is organised as follows: Section II briefly describes the relevant regulations and antitrust law as they applied to airlines before 1978 and the changes since deregulation. Section III provides a detailed discussion of the economic issues that are important in assessing the costs and benefits of deregulation. A summary and conclusions are contained in Section IV.

II. SUMMARY OF REGULATORY FRAMEWORK AND APPLICATION
OF ANTITRUST LAWS

A. Regulation prior to 1978

3.   Prior to 1978, the Civil Aeronautic Boards (CAB) was the US regulatory agency with authority over airlines. The Board controlled entry into new and existing routes, controlled the exit of carriers from routes, regulated fares, awarded direct subsidies to air carriers, and controlled mergers and intercarrier agreements, thus immunizing carriers from the antitrust laws.

4.   Routes were almost always granted to existing carriers after lengthy and complex proceedings, with the Board usually rejecting applications to start new airlines. The Board's policies also restricted entry into markets

where there was an incumbent carrier. Competitive routes were only awarded when it was determined that entry would not significantly erode the incumbent's profits.

5.   The CAB's focus in regulating fares was on overall industry profitability rather than on the relationship between price and cost. The Board also provided subsidies for a group of regional carriers to protect service to small communities. In evaluating mergers, the Board was most concerned with whether the newly consolidated carrier would divert traffic and revenue from competing carriers.

6.   It should be noted that the CAB's regulatory authority extended only over interstate airlines. Many studies showed that unregulated intrastate carriers were operating at lower fares than carriers operating on similar interstate routes. These studies were probably the greatest stimulus for reform of the CAB regulatory framework (1). While academic studies laid the groundwork for change, the Board itself began to question the desirability of its regulatory activities in 1977. With political support galvanized by Senator Edward Kennedy's hearings on airlines in 1975, the Airline Deregulation Act (ADA) was enacted in 1978.

B. Regulation after 1978

7.   The Airline Deregulation Act of 1978 imposed a gradual reduction in the Civil Aeronautics Board's regulation of the air transport industry. After 1981, CAB authority over routes ended; on January 1, 1983 its authority over rates, mergers and acquisitions was terminated. The Board ceased all regulatory operations at the end of 1984. Regulation of air safety remained in the hands of the Federal Aviation Administration and was not affected by the ADA.

8.   All remaining responsibilities for overseeing the airline industry were transferred to the Department of Transportation (DOT). These responsibilities include:

1. Negotiating international agreements between carriers;

2. Overseeing the local service subsidy programme. The programme of subsidies to carriers serving low-density routes was continued to assuage fears that service to small communities would disappear under deregulation. This programme, scheduled to end in 1988, provides subsidies to carriers that provide service to each of 150 communities;

3. Approving all mergers between carriers. Although DOT must approve mergers, the airlines are still subject to the full weight of the US Antitrust Laws. Exemptions occur only if DOT grants immunity to a particular merger or other carrier agreement. DOT's authority over mergers and powers to grant immunity expires in 1989.

III. OVERVIEW OF US EXPERIENCE WITH DEREGULATION

A. Routes

9.   Since 1982, entry into airline markets has been open to all carriers that are willing and able. Existing air carriers have complete freedom to abandon or add routes as they see fit. Prior to deregulation, competition for route authority was strictly controlled by the CAB, with usually only one or two carriers being granted authority on all but the most dense routes. As a result, routes became a scarce commodity with substantial economic rents accruing to those carriers with route certificates. These rents were dissipated, in part, however, through the administrative costs of participating in a CAB route proceeding. Deregulation has eliminated those costs, and through competition, eliminated the scarcity value of most routes.

10.   The most significant result of route deregulation has been the accelerated development of hub-and-spoke route structures. A hub system feeds passengers from various cities into a centralised airport (hub), where they connect to other flights for destinations beyond the hub. The economic rationale for hub operations arises from the airlines' ability to take advantage of economies of scope. Firms benefit from economies of scope when the cost of joint production of two outputs is less than the cost of producing each output separately. In the case of airlines, it may be less costly for a carrier to combine passengers from one city who wish to travel to several destinations onto a single large aircraft with connections at a hub, rather than to schedule non-stop flights from one city to all desired destinations using smaller airplanes.

11.   These cost savings will occur when economies of aircraft size exceed the cost of rerouting traffic through a complex hub. Economies of aircraft size arise because a hubbing carrier serves more passengers on its flights, allowing it to use larger aircraft at higher load factors: the carrier will therefore increase the average number of passengers per flight and reduce costs. The costs of rerouting traffic include decreased demand from passengers for connecting flights and the more complex handling facilities necessary at a hub. Economies of scope appear to be significant as most carriers have accelerated the development of hub operations since deregulation.

12.   In assessing the benefits of "hubbing", the savings in resources to the firm must be traded off against the effect on passenger convenience and flying time. Passengers from small communities appear to have benefited from the new configuration because of the increased likelihood that they will be able to make co-ordinated connections on one carrier from their origin to their destination; before deregulation, unco-ordinated interline connections were more likely (2). This is a real savings to consumers as it reduces travel time and reduces the chances that baggage will be lost or connections will be missed.

13.   As was expected, the effect on the number of departures has been mixed. Bailey, Graham and Kaplan found that service to large hubs from all destinations has increased, while non-stop service between non-hub cities and small hubs has declined. At this time, however, the percentage of passengers

107

requiring connections has not increased (3). Also, Morrison and Winston have found that because a high percentage of business travellers are flying to and from large hubs, they have benefited greatly from increased flight frequency (4). These gains are due to the high value business travellers place on their ability to find a flight closest to their desired departure time.

14. The development of hub configurations has and will have a significant impact on competition. Although the benefit of hub networks were known before deregulation, many thought that only the largest carriers would benefit from these economies. Their domination of the long distance routes suggested that large carriers could funnel passengers from smaller routes also served by small regional carriers onto their own aircraft, thus making it difficult for the smaller carriers to compete. Not foreseen, however, was that the smaller carriers already dominated feed traffic in many regions of the US, and with their emerging ability to enter more heavily travelled routes, could profit greatly from a hub structure. Thus, the local carriers were significant winners, in term of profitability, from deregulation (5).

15. The effect of deregulation on new carrier entry still remains an open question. Although entry into any one city pair appears easy, carriers are operating integrated route networks, and thus the viability of any single route will be related to the carriers ability to develop other routes. To compete with a carrier who already has a hub at a particular city, for example, entry into a significant portion of the spoke routes may be required. Such an undertaking may be costly in terms of the number of planes required and in terms of the fixed costs of developing a passenger following. In that case, hubs may create a barrier to entry, allowing incumbent firms to charge higher prices without fear of immediate entry.

B. Fares

16. Since 1983, carriers have had complete flexibility to set passenger fares. Before deregulation, the CAB set fares on the basis of distance. Unfortunately, strict regulation prevented fares from falling to reflect the cost savings of new aircraft. Competition, it was predicted, would reduce the incentive to engage in wasteful service competition, lower fares and benefit consumers.

17. Under regulation, as new and more efficient aircraft were developed, air fares deviated more and more from the true costs of service. Unable to compete on the basis of price in markets where price was set above cost, the airlines engaged in a form of nonprice competition; increasing flight frequency and lowering load factors. Thus, all profits were dissipated in the form of wasteful service competition.

18. In short haul markets, prices were set below costs, leading to an insufficient allocation of aircraft resources and high load factors. As was found by Douglas and Miller, there existed an inverse relationship between distance and load factor (6). Because the structure of fares did not represent the structure of costs, excess capacity was more pronounced in long haul markets than in short haul markets.

19.   In general, costs depend on the distance travelled and the volume of passengers in the market. Costs are lowered when larger aircrafts are run at higher load factors. Of course, pure cost minimization will not maximize profits as carriers must account for passenger convenience, trading off load factor with the demand for flight frequency. Deregulation allowed carriers to make these choices, along with setting fares.

20.   The difference in costs across markets is mostly due to economies of scale. As the volume of passengers in a market increases, carriers will substitute larger aircraft instead of increasing flight frequency, since the demand for flight frequency does not increase proportionally with the number of passengers. Also, in the longer distance markets, large aircraft are more efficient, and can be run at higher load factors because passengers are less willing to substitute other modes of transportation for air travel. Thus, an efficient use of resources would demand higher load factors and increased equipment size as distance and density increased. The study by Bailey, Graham and Kaplan showed this to be true; thus, deregulation has forced a reversal of the inefficiencies documented by Douglas and Miller.

21.   The consensus in the literature on deregulation is that competition has brought fares in line with these resource costs. Average fares have fallen on long-haul routes, but have risen on short-haul routes. Across all the markets there are various passenger groups that can be considered winners and losers, however. Recent studies by Moore and by Morrison and Winston show that the average unrestricted coach fares have risen, while average discount fares have declined. For example, in their study of 812 city pairs, Morrison and Winston find that coach fares increased 10.3 per cent, while discount fares decreased 15.3 per cent (7). Thus, travellers who tend to fly unrestricted fares have not benefited from deregulation, in terms of fares, while the majority of passengers, who pay discount fares, have on average benefited.

22.   Moore's study produces unclear results, although he points out that a similar relationship between changes in coach and discount fares is most evident in long-haul routes (8). It must be kept in mind, however, that long-haul travel is significantly more important to travellers than short haul. In Moore's study, for example, nearly 90 per cent of passengers were flying in long haul markets.

23.   If one accounts for improvements in flight frequencies as well as fare changes the benefits from deregulation are overwhelmingly positive in the aggregate. Morrison and Winston have estimated that when the changes in fares, flight frequency and time of travel are combined, the total benefit to consumers has been $5.7 billion annually (9). These benefits have been distributed across all markets except the least dense short distance markets.

C. Industry structure and competition

24.   Critics of deregulation predicted that unfettered competition would lead to a major consolidation within the industry. They feared that in the long run a handful of firms would dominate the industry, causing fares to increase above regulated levels. Other experts countered that the threat of entry into airline markets by new and established carriers would force incumbents to hold fares at competitive levels. Even with economies of scale

and a small number of firms in each market, airline markets would behave like competitive markets. Thus, the question of how concentration and entry affect the level of fares is crucial for assessing the long run consequences of deregulation for consumer welfare. In this section, we describe briefly the character of entry since deregulation, and then examine the current results on the relationship between market structure and fares.

25.   Entry can take the form of a new airline establishing a presence in a city-pair or an established carrier expanding its route network. Several new carriers have started service since 1979, including Midway, New York Air and People Express. The primary source of advantage for new entrants has been their ability to escape from non-competitive labour practices inherited from the regulated era. New carriers have substantial cost advantages, creating pressure on incumbents to also reduce costs. Note that although mismanagement may have lead to the bankruptcy of Braniff Airlines, the problem of widespread bankruptcies has not occurred in the deregulated period.

26.   In his study, Moore examined the phenomenon of expanded route systems by established airlines. Using a sample of city-pairs of varying sizes he found that the percentage of cities gaining carriers exceeded the percentage that lost carriers in all size categories. While the sample is small, expansion into competitors routes seems to have occurred rapidly since 1978.

27.   Given the evidence on entry, it appears that airline markets are highly competitive, despite the fact that these markets are concentrated relative to other industries. Recently, several studies have been completed that analyse more closely the issue of how market structure affects fares. Specifically, they ask the question does the apparently easy entry into airline markets have a downward effect on fares?

28.   One particular working hypothesis has been that airline markets are "contestable". A market is contestable when a firm could prospectively shift assets into a market where prices are above cost, while recovering all his fixed costs if he exits the market. If that is the case, then actual entry should not affect prices; only the threat of entry should matter. Any attempt by an incumbent to raise price would be met immediately by competitive entry. If in fact only the threat of entry would keep fares at competitive levels, then the level of concentration should not have a direct impact on fares. Even markets with only one firm would price competitively. Although this scenario may appear unrealistic, an imperfect version may hold in an industry where assets are highly mobile, such as airlines (10).

29.   The alternative to this theory is that there are certain costs in terms of time and money that a carrier must incur to establish its reputation among a group of passengers. For example, advertising is necessary to inform customers. At the same time, established carriers may hold certain loyalty advantages, such as a large route network and a frequent flyer programme, which may increase the time an entrant needs to make a competitive impact. Thus, incumbent carriers may be able to profitably hold price above cost without immediately losing market share to entrants. The ability to sustain these high prices may well increase as the level concentration of the incumbent carriers rises. A reduced number of competitors will be able to act as an interdependent oligopoly and co-ordinate pricing.

30.   There may be certain other barriers to entry as well. In the section on routes above, we discussed how a hub structure may make competitive entry more difficult. This will be especially true at airports that have a constrained level of capacity, thus making it difficult for new entrants to mount the large number of flights necessary to compete with a hub carrier. Even with deregulation, some carriers may have a particular route system and geographic location which could give them the power to raise price above cost.

31.   Research on fares and market structures has been quite extensive. The general conclusions have been that increases in concentration do lead to increases in fares (11).   Thus, the contestable market hypothesis, which states that the actual number of competitors is irrelevant, has been generally rejected.

32.   However, there is support for the hypothesis that fares have gradually declined on high density routes into which new and existing firms have entered. Entry of existing large carriers has been found to have an especially large negative impact on fares on these routes (12).   Their ability to match an incumbent carrier's reputation advantage probably explains this phenomenon. In general, the large airlines have not lowered fares as quickly when faced with entry by a low cost airline that promotes itself as a discount carrier. Instead, a two-tier pricing system is usually employed by the large carrier in which lower fares are only available on a fixed number of seats.

33.   It is important to remember that these conclusions are based on only short-run trends. In the long run, the new entrants may be able to match the reputation advantages of the incumbents. When that occurs, the airline industry will become even more competitive.

D. Factors of production

34.   As discussed in the sections on routes and fares, airline deregulation in the US has led to substantial efficiency gains. The question arises, however, whether specific groups have been adversely affected in the transition from a deregulated structure to an unregulated equilibrium. A great majority of passengers have benefited due to lower fares. In this section, we analyse the impact of deregulation on labour and on capital.

1. Labour

35.   Predicting the long run effect of deregulation on the airline labour force is difficult. The Mutual Aid Pact, a feature of the regulated period, whereby airlines whose workers engaged in a strike shared the revenues of working airlines, has been eliminated. Unions now have greater bargaining power, with carriers more vulnerable to strikes. On the other hand, with deregulated fares, carriers have greater incentives to cut costs. Because bargaining is carrier specific, unions of that carrier have a greater incentive to undercut wages of other carrier's unions to give their carrier an advantage in their market, and add to their own job security. Although the final outcome for labour is uncertain, some preliminary conclusions can be made based on the changes in employment and wage rates between the period

before and after deregulation. These data are not necessarily conclusive, however, because fuel price increases and recessions have had an effect on labour which must be disentangled from the effects of competition.

36.   The study by Morrison and Winston shows that real airline wages were slightly higher (1.8 per cent) in 1983 than in 1977, while real wages in the private sector in general fell 9.4 per cent (13). Moore computes a real increase in airline labour costs of 8.3 per cent between 1976 and 1983, also suggesting some gains for labour (14). Moreover, the level of airline employment increased by 9 per cent between 1976 and 1982 (15).

37.   Although these data paint a sanguine picture of labour's prospects, the figures are somewhat misleading. New carriers are entering the industry with nonunion labour forces. According to Moore there have been fourteen such entrants since deregulation (16). This has weakened the bargaining power of labour, leading in many cases to wage concessions to established carriers. The increased entry may, however, lead to further increases in employment.

38.   Several of the major US carriers now have two-tier wage structures, under which new employees are paid less than workers hired before negotiation of the new contracts. People Express has developed a unique incentive system in which workers are required to purchase shares of stock in the airline. With wage patterns still in transition, however, the long run effect on the welfare of labour is unclear.

2. Capital

39.   At the time of deregulation, US carriers were divided into two groups. Trunk carriers operated either nationally or over large areas of the country, while regional carriers operated in well-defined geographic areas and were the beneficiaries of subsidies to serve small communities. With varying endowments prior to deregulation, the differential impact on specific carriers was likely to be substantial. In the long run, however, the ability of established airlines to take advantage of rents accruing from first mover advantages should be dissipated by new entry.

40.   Bailey and Williams have analysed the patterns of airline profit margins in a recent study. They found a statistically significant difference in the mean level of returns for regional and trunk carriers between 1978 and 1984. The pattern of returns of over time also differs quite markedly, with regional carriers earning steady profits, while trunk carriers as a whole experiencing a drop and then a recovery in profits. Similarly, they tested to see if the two carriers with the largest national market share, United and American, had a pattern of returns different from the other trunks. Here too they found a statistically different pattern of returns, with the two largest carriers recovering much faster from the shock of deregulation than the other trunks. The mean returns, however, were not significantly different (17).

41.   Essentially, the two large trunks made use of scale based advantages. They succeeded in counteracting the notion that air service is a commodity, perfectly substitutable between carriers, by differentiating their products. Thus, such volume-based innovations as frequent flyer plans and computer reservation systems helped sustain demand for their services. The other

trunks did not innovate as quickly because of fewer scale advantages and were situated in hub cities that were not as advantageously located as the two largest carriers. Also, as mentioned earlier, the regional carriers had great success in creating regional hubs via the feeder routes they inherited from the regulated era.

42.   Another measure of benefits to capital are changes in stock valuation. Calculations done by Moore show almost no change in the total value of stock for the trunk carriers as a whole between 1976 and 1983. On the other hand, the market evaluation of the regional carriers increased six-fold over the same period (18). The market has confirmed the patterns of profits in the industry, predicting that in the short run the regional carriers, on average, have been the beneficiaries of the returns from deregulation.

E. Other issues

1. Safety

43.   Airline safety continues to be regulated by Federal Aviation Administration. Their authority was not affected by the airline deregulation act. Many feared that competition among airlines, and the consequent incentives to reduce costs, might cause the carriers to compromise safety to gain a competitive advantage. There is no evidence that this has occurred, and in fact the average accident rate has declined 28 per cent since 1978 (19).

44.   Clearly, the safety performance of an industry is, in part, a result of economic decisions made by the firms in the industry: e.g., the amount of money spent on maintenance and employee training. There may be feedback effects on safety from the increased price competition and entry caused by economic deregulation. On the other hand, the market itself may provide carriers with the incentives to operate safely. Although carriers can insure against most of their losses, they cannot insure against loss in demand that may result if consumers view a carrier's accident as important information about their safety level.

45.   Several empirical studies have been done that study the link between airline safety and economic deregulation. Oster and Zorn (20) find very little evidence supporting any degradation in safety. In the area of commuter airlines they find that there has not been a substantial reduction in safety for travelers to and from small communities. Second, for both commuter and jet carriers, the rates for accidents related to equipment failure are substantially lower in the post-deregulation period. This suggests that, at least through 1985, there is no evidence of increased accidents from worsening maintenance practices. Third, despite the increase in hub and spoke operations, and the increase in pressure they cause on the air traffic control system, the rate of air traffic control related accidents is lower in the post-deregulation period than prior to deregulation.

46.   Kanafani and Keeler (21) also looked at the question of safety and deregulation. They studied a panel of jet-operating airlines, including new entrants since deregulation and large, established carriers in existence over several decades. Overall, the results indicate that the new carriers studied

have safety records just as strong as those of the established carriers. By some measures incumbents are safer than new entrants, and by other measures the reverse is true. However, in all cases, the differences between the two carrier groups are statistically insignificant.

47.   While more empirical work needs to be done, early research seems to indicate that the fears of serious safety degradation brought on by deregulation are unfounded.

2. Mergers

48.   The Airline Deregulation Act directed the Board and subsequently the Department of Transportation to apply the standards of Section 7 of the Clayton Antitrust Act when evaluating mergers. The agencies were to determine whether the merger would lead to a substantial increase in market power and thus, the ability to profitably raise prices for a significant length of time.

49.   Currently, the process of merger approval begins with a hearing before an administrative law judge at the DOT. At these hearings interested parties may provide evidence and testimony for or against the acquisition. The traditional antitrust authority, the US Department of Justice, is usually a major participant in these proceedings. Once the judge has made a recommendation, the Secretary of Transportation makes the final determination.

50.   Several factors are particularly relevant for making these decisions. First, it must be determined in what relevant market the merger is likely to reduce competition. Second, the change in market shares must be examined as an indication of reduced competition. Third, attention should be focused on the ability of actual and potential competitors to check the exercise of market power over price. The number of carriers adequately situated to enter easily and the ability to gain access to an airport are particularly important. Last, the possible efficiencies from the merger may also be considered in the analysis. Part two of this paper provides an extensive discussion of recent merger cases.

3. Airline computer reservation systems

51.   The proliferation of fares and schedules under deregulation has raised the possibility that the allocation of passengers and routes will be distorted because of incomplete information. To provide better information, several of the carriers, including United and American, have developed computer reservation systems from which travel agents can sell tickets on the vendor's airline as well as on the other airlines that participate in the system.

52.   Unfortunately, it has been found that much of the information displayed via these systems was biased in favor of the carrier who owned the system. The Department of Justice investigated these allegations in 1983, recommending to the CAB that rules be adopted to prevent bias. Anti-bias rules were promulgated in 1984. In 1985, the Department of Justice found that bias had been virtually eliminated (22).

53.   In addition to bias, the question of how carriers who owned CRS's were setting the price of access to the system by other carriers also arose. Since a carrier had to participate in all the available systems to reach a broad group of travel agents, the opportunity for carrier/vendors to exercise market power against specific rival carriers was substantial. The Department of Justice recommended that CAB wait for the outcome of the antibias rules before regulating prices. The CAB, however, decided to institute immediately a non-discriminatory price rule in which vendors could charge any price for access, but the price charged had to be the same for all participants.

54.   The competitive effects of bias and monopoly access pricing are clear. By selectively disadvantaging carriers with bias, and by increasing their rivals' cost relative to their own via supracompetitive access prices, the vendor can decrease competition in the air transportation market.

IV. SUMMARY AND CONCLUSIONS

55.   Although the legislative process of airline deregulation is now complete, the industry remains in a transition phase. Carriers are continuing to expand and reorganize their route structures into hub configurations, resulting in a more efficient use of aircraft resources, as well as improved convenience for a broader spectrum of air travellers. Deregulation has also given the carriers complete flexibility to adjust their fares. There is strong evidence that deregulation has brought fares more in line with the true cost of providing service, a structure quite different from what existed in the regulated period.

56.   With complete flexibility in adjusting routes and fares, it was hoped that competition on any given air route would lead carriers to reduce fares, with competitors undercutting any attempts to charge supracompetitive prices. However, the transition to deregulation has not produced large numbers of carriers competing on all routes. Technological characteristics of aircraft, specifically scale economies, have led to high levels of concentration on all but a small number of routes. Economies are especially prevalent on long-haul or long distance routes. Thus, the problem of oligopolistic interdependence and the ability to co-ordinate pricing remains a real fear under deregulation.

57.   Many economists hypothesized that although there were economies of aircraft size and economies of scale in route networks, the mere threat of entering into a city-pair market by a carrier operating at the same low cost level as an incumbent would induce the incumbent carriers to set fares closer to competitive levels. Thus, even with some economies of scale, airline markets would behave like competitive markets, independent of the number of firms, and fares would fall. Various studies have shown, however, that this contestability scenario has not materialised, and only actual entry has a downward effect on fares (23). Thus, significant increases in concentration within city-pair markets could make fares sticky downward, affecting consumer welfare adversely. In general, however, research shows that, on average, fares have fallen; in particular, declines have occurred on routes where economies are most prevalent, such as long-haul markets, and also on dense routes with high load factors.

58.   Along with the positive economic question of how deregulation has affected consumer welfare, there are distributional questions of how deregulation has affected factors of production, i.e. labour and capital. It appears that deregulation has not had an adverse impact on labour up to this point. Employment levels are up and average wages have remained relatively stable. In the long run, however, new carriers not bound by long-term labour contracts are expected to act as lower cost competitors for the incumbent airlines, forcing the overall wage level in the industry downward.

59.   Changes in the stock market's evaluation of the US carriers since deregulation clearly shows a strong pattern of winners and losers among firms.   In general, the two largest full service or trunk carriers (United Airlines and American Airlines) and the former regional carriers have all benefited from deregulation in the eyes of the market.   The other trunk carriers have not faired nearly as well in terms of stock market valuation. The success of a specific set of carriers seems to have been caused primarily by their ability to utilize effectively route endowments and to preserve passenger loyalty that they inherited from the regulated period.

60.   Three other issues, although closely linked with the allocative and distributional questions outlined above, are worth mentioning separately. First, deregulation does not appear to have created a reduction in air safety.   The FAA continues to regulate in this area.   Second, the US air carriers are now subject fully to all the applicable antitrust laws. A policy towards mergers set by the Department of Transportation will have a profound effect on the long-run consequences of deregulation for competition in air transport.   Third, airline computerized reservation system (CRS) have become a powerful marketing tool for a few of the larger carriers. Since a travel agent's reservation is an important input to the production of air transportation services, it is possible that these systems could be used to restrict competition. Currently, new rules promulgated by the CAB before it ceased operations at the end of 1984 have placed some restrictions on the ability of carriers owners of CRS systems to manipulate their systems in an anticompetitive manner.

61.   In conclusion, the consequences of deregulation in the US airline sector appear to be mainly beneficial. There are four main results. First, the competitive market mechanism has forced a more efficient allocation of airline resources and an expanded array of price/quality options.   Second, fares have declined on long-haul routes, but increased on short-haul routes. With the majority of passengers travelling in the longer markets, the average fare paid has declined. At the same time, business travellers have benefited from increased flight frequency.   Third, stockholders of airlines have generally benefited, but new employees of the airlines are receiving lower wages than employees hired previously. Employment, however, has increased. Last, new carrier entry appears to be checking the market power of incumbent airlines.

NOTES AND REFERENCES

1. For a summary of the various studies, see Bailey, E. Graham, D. And Kaplan, D. Deregulating the Airlines, Cambridge, Mass. MIT Press, 1985, pp. 26-28.

2. Morrison, S. and Winston, C., The Economic Effects of Airline Deregulation, Washington, DC: Brookings Institution, 1986, pp. 8-9.

3. Bailey, Graham and Kaplan, Op.cit., p. 119.

4. Morrison and Winston, Op.cit., pp. 25-26.

5. For an interesting discussion of the strategy used by the local service carriers see Bailey, E. and Williams, J., "Sources of Economic Rent in the Deregulated Airline Industry", Graduate School of Industrial Administration, Carnegie-Mellon University, March, 1986.

6. Douglas, G. and Miller, J. Economic Regulation of Domestic Air Transport: Theory and Policy, Washington, D.C.: Brookings Institution, 1974.

7. Morrison and Winston, Op.cit., p. 22.

8. Moore, T., "US Airline Deregulation: Its Effects on Passengers, Capital and Labor," Journal of Law and Economics, April 1986, pp. 1-29.

9. Morrison and Winston, Op.cit., pp. 25-33. For purposes of their study Morrison and Winston used the changes in feasible flight departure alternatives as a measure of frequency in each city-pair. The change in sceduled travel time is included in the computations to account for the effects of hubbing and other changes in route structure. They use wages as a proxy for passengers' value of time.

10. See, for example, Bailey, E. and Panzar, J. "The Contestability of Airline Markets during the Transition to Deregulation", Journal of Law and Contemporary Problems, Winter 1981, pp. 125-145; a full discussion of contestability is contained in Baumol, W.J., Panzer, J. and Willig, R. Contestable Markets and the Theory of Industry Strcture, New York: Harcourt, Brace, Jovanovich, Inc., 1982.

11. Examples are:

    -- Bailey, Graham and Kaplan, Op. cit., chap. 9;

    -- Moore, Op. cit., p.16-23;

-- Morrison and Winston, Op. cit., chap. 5;

-- Call, G. and Keeler, T.: "Airline Deregulation, Fares and Market Behavior; Some Empirical Evidence" in Andrew F. Daughety, Ed. Analytical Studies in Transport Economics. London: Cambridge University Press, 1985.

-- Williams, M., Joskow, A., Johnson, R. and Hurdle, G. "Explaining and Predicting Airline Yields with Non-Parametric Regression Trees." Economics Letters, Vol. 24, pp. 99-108.

-- Hurdle, G., Johnson, R., Joskow, A., Werder, G. and Williams, M. "Concentration, Potential Entry, and Performance in the Airline Industry," paper presented at the Southern Economics Association meetings, Washington, DC, November 1987.

12.   Call and Keeler, Op.cit., p. 37.

13.   Morrison and Winston, Op.cit., p. 43.

14.   Moore, Op.cit., p. 25.

15.   Ibid., p. 25-26.

16.   Ibid., p. 25.

17.   Bailey and Williams, Op.cit., p. 3-5.

18.   Moore, Op.cit., pp. 23-24.

19.   See "An Interview with Elizabeth Dole", District Lawyer March/April 1986, p. 37-41.

20.   Clinton V. Oster, Jr. and C. Kurt Zorn (1987), "Airline Deregulation: Is it Still Safe to Fly?" paper presented at Transportation Deregulation and Safety Conference, Northwestern University, June 1987.

21.   A. Kanafani and T.E. Keeler (1987), "New Entrants and Safety: Some Statistical Evidence on the Effects of Airline Deregulation," paper presented at Transportation Deregulation and Safety Conference, Northwestern University, June 1987.

22.   See US Department of Justice, 1985 Report of the Department of Justice to Congress on the Airline Computer Reservation System Industry, Dec. 20, 1985.

23.   For references see note 11, above.

Part Two

DEREGULATION IN THE US AIR TRANSPORT SECTOR
-- RECENT DEVELOPMENTS 1985-1987

I. MERGERS

A. Introduction

62.   Since deregulation in 1978, the US domestic airline sector has experienced a simultaneous expansion and consolidation. At the time of deregulation, there were 36 certificated carriers, while today there are 74 certificated carriers. However, the latter figure may overstate the extent of competition: 49 of the carriers operate entirely outside of the 48 contiguous states or have "feeder" agreements with larger carriers, leaving 25 independent competitors in the Continental US. Table 1 lists these 25 carriers separated into three categories: Major, National, and Regional carriers. Note that, in the absence of any consolidations or exits from the industry there would now be over 200 carriers. The pace of consolidation has been particularly rapid since late 1985, a period during which there were 23 acquisitions by large carriers.

63.   On an overall nationwide basis the industry has become significantly more concentrated. In January 1986, there were thirteen carriers with annual revenues of over $1 billion; by February 1987 there were only nine airlines in this category. Table 2 shows the top ten airlines ranked by revenue passenger miles as of March 1987. The top four carriers account for about 60 per cent of the total revenue passenger miles.

64.   It is important not to misinterpret these figures as indicating the failure of deregulation to preserve competition. National concentration figures do not capture well the nature of competition in this industry. If for example, one used national concentration figures to evaluate the merger between Northwest Airlines and Republic Airlines, one would have concluded that it did not violate the Department of Justice's Merger Guidelines, even though competition on a substantial number of city pairs was significantly affected by the merger. Future study, based on more current data, needs to be done to confirm that these conclusions still hold.

65.   Under the current view, competition among carriers takes place in the provision of air transportation on specific city pairs. On average, there are more carriers on city pairs than there were before deregulation and carriers are providing more service. The studies cited in part one, especially those by Moore (1), and by Morrison and Winston (2) support these conclusions. Section C below addresses the issue of whether the recent round of consolidations has changed the conditions necessary for successful competitive entry.

Table 1

INDEPENDENT CARRIERS OPERATING

January 1987

Majors (9)	Nationals (5)	Regionals (11)
American	Alaska	Air Nevada
Delta	Braniff	Challenge Air
Northwest	Hawaiian	Florida Express
Pan American	Midway	Jet Express
Piedmont	Southwest	McClaim
Texas Air Corp.		Midwest & Express
Trans World		Sky Star
United		Statewest
USAir		Sunworld International
		Tower Air

66.   Section B provides a brief synopsis of some of the major acquisition cases that have come before the Department of Transportation (DOT) in the last two years (3). Many of the economic issues discussed in section III C of part one were crucial in determining the outcome of the cited cases. For the most part, parties to the proceedings disagreed on the proper definition of the relevant market and on the likelihood of entry. Also, in the face of substantial empirical evidence to the contrary, some parties remained convinced that the mere threat of entry would prevent anticompetitive performance even in highly concentrated markets.

B. Economic Analysis of Significant Merger Cases 1985-1987

1. Pacific Division Transfer Case

67.   In April 1985 United Airlines offered to buy Pan American's Pacific Division. The Department of Justice (DOJ) filed a brief stating that they were opposed to the transaction unless United agreed to spin off one gateway to Tokyo from the West Coast of the United States. With a reduction in the number of US carriers in the Pacific from three to two (Northwest Airlines was also a carrier), and with the restrictions on entry and capacity dictated by the US-Japan bilaterals, DOJ felt the transfer would strengthen the IATA fare cartel.

Table 2

INDUSTRY MARKET SHARE
Revenue Passenger Miles (000)

Company Name	RPM's	% Share
1. Texas Air System	61,322,216	21.69
2. United	45,458,375	16.08
3. American & Air Cal	43,479,472	15.38
4. Delta & Western	37,867,779	13.39
5. Northwest & Republic	23,109,799	8.17
6. TWA & Ozark	18,745,975	6.63
7. USAir & PSA	13,673,229	4.84
8. Piedmont	9,320,681	3.30
9. Southwest/Transtar	6,642,359	2.35
10.Pan American	4,853,671	1.72
TOTAL:	250,727,581	80.16
INDUSTRY TOTAL:	282,743,626	100.00

Source: Aviation Daily, April 16, 1987 and Department of Justice Calculations.

Notes:

1. Texas Air System includes Continental and Eastern Airlines.

2. American's purchase of Air Cal was approved by DOT on March 30, 1987. Delta's purchase of Western was approved by DOT on December 11, 1986. USAIR's purchase of Pacific Southwest (PSA) was approved on March 4, 1987. All other acquisitions are discussed in the text.

3. The proposed merger of USAIR and Piedmont is now pending at the Department of Transportation.

68.   The Department of Transportation agreed that there may be some loss of competition due to the transfer, but felt that it was not likely to be substantial. In particular, they pointed to a new Memorandum of Understanding between the United States and Japan that would allow new entry in the Pacific market in 1986. DOT also agreed to authorise a future proceeding to determine if another carrier should be chosen to replace United in the Seattle-Tokyo market. Subsequently, and in keeping with the Memorandum of Understanding, American Airlines, Delta Airlines, and a new Japanese Carrier (ANA) were given gateways to Tokyo. The Seattle proceedings are currently under way.

2. Northwest Airlines Acquisition of Republic Airlines

69.   Northwest Airlines filed an application with DOT in January 1986 for permission to merge with Republic Airlines. Both carriers had major hub operations in Minneapolis and were head-to-head competitors on 45 city pairs. The combined carrier would control 80 per cent of the gates at the Minneapolis airport. There was also substantial competition between the two airlines in Detroit. The Department of Justice opposed the combination on the grounds that the acquisition was likely to reduce competition in nonstop city-pair markets to and from Minneapolis. As discussed in part one, there are substantial economies in running a complete hub operation. DOJ argued that for a new carrier to discipline the market power of the combined airline it would have to enter with a complete hub operation. The Department felt that this was unlikely even in the face of increased fares on the part of Northwest-Republic. DOT disagreed, concluding that the markets cited by DOJ received sufficient competition from one-stop service, connecting service, new entrants, and other forms of service.

3. TWA acquisition of Ozark Airlines

70.   TWA and Ozark applied for permission to merge in March 1986, soon after the Northwest/Republic application. The competitive issues in the TWA acquisition were quite similar to those in the Northwest acquisition. Both TWA and Ozark had substantial hub operations at St. Louis, with the combined carriers controlling 76 per cent of the gates. Again the Department of Justice focussed on nonstop city pairs from the hub as being the markets in which anticompetitive results might occur after the merger. DOJ reiterated the point that there was little chance of entry because of a need for a hub. Their position was that ten gates should be spun-off at the St. Louis airport to allow new entry. The Transportation Department disagreed again and approved the merger in September 1986 (4).

4. Texas Air Acquisition of Eastern Airlines

71.   The competition issues raised in the takeover of Eastern Airlines were substantially different from the concerns in the earlier mergers between carriers with overlapping hubs. In this case, the area of substantial concern was competition in the Northeast corridor of the United States. Two routes, Washington-New York and Boston-New York, created special problems. Both routes are heavily dominated by business travellers. Typically, business travellers are time-sensitive and view frequent service as the most important

factor in determining which airline to choose. Two airlines, Eastern and New York Air (a Texas Air subsidiary), were direct competitors in these two city pairs for the provision of hourly shuttle service. While other carriers provided irregular service on the two routes, only the merging carriers provided shuttle service between the airports closest to the downtown areas in New York and Washington, as well as at Boston. Thus, there was a substantial possibility that airport pairs represented a relevant market. If so, the proposed combination would have eliminated all existing competition.

72.   The question of whether another carrier would enter the shuttle business in response to the merged carrier's attempt to raise price was complicated in this case because access to the close-in airports, LaGuardia in New York and National in Washington, is restricted. In order to operate at one of these airports a carrier must own a licence, or "slot", that gives them the right to take off or land in a particular hour. Although carriers can buy and sell slots, it was clear that a new carrier contemplating entry would require a substantial number of these slots throughout the day to offer a competitive shuttle service (5).

73.   To alleviate this problem, and avoid a protracted investigation, Texas Air offered to sell a large number of these slots to Pan American Airways, who would then operate a competing shuttle service. Even so, the Department of Transportaion disapproved the transacation, stating that the number of slots offered to Pan Am was not adequate to guarantee a viable shuttle service. Texas Air subsequently resolved these objections by selling Pan Am more slots. The merger was approved on October 1, 1986 (6).

5. Texas Air acquisition of People Express

74.   People Express was one of the most celebrated examples of deregulation's benefits. The carrier had established a hub at Newark's underutilised airport outside of New York City. By offering unrestricted low fares to a large number of locations, the carrier developed a demand for air travel among people who otherwise might not have travelled by air. People Express also showed how new entry could affect the prices of incumbent carriers. However, the airline started to experience significant financial difficulties in early 1986. In September 1986, they agreed to a buyout proposal by Texas Air.

75.   The economic analysis of this case focused on many of the scale and density issues discussed in section III B of part one. People Express operated a hub at Newark, while Texas Air's subsidiary, New York Air did not. Both carriers, however, were carrying primarily local traffic on their routes out of Newark, with People Express generating very little traffic from locations beyond the hub. A lack of beyond traffic is considered strong evidence that a hub network is not crucial for operating competitive service. This, along with the high density of traffic on the overlapping routes, made entry by a new carrier on a point-to-point basis without a hub likely in response to a price increase by the combined carrier. Thus, any attempt to exercise market power would be kept in check.

76.   On October 1, 1986 the Department of Justice conveyed its opinion to the Department of Transportation that "the proposed acquisition is not likely to lessen competition substantially." DOT gave final approval on October 24, 1986.

6.   USAir Group Acquisition of Piedmont

77.   In March 1987, USAir offered to acquire Piedmont Aviation. Both airlines are East Coast carriers. Although USAir operated primarily in the Northeast and Piedmont operated primarily in the Southeast, there nonetheless was competitive overlap. As in the acquisition of Eastern Airlines by Texas Air, the control of slots at LaGuardia and National airports was a central issue. In this case the analysis focused on the effects of concentrated slot holdings on fares to and from these airports. Also, the availability of alternative connecting service on north-south routes after the merger became a competitive issue. The analysis of this question focused on the availability of alternative connecting hubs, and the likelihood that new hubs would be built.

78.   The Department of Justice concluded that "it could not establish that the merger owuld eliminate substantial competition". A Phoenix, Arizona-based airline, America West, which was seeking slots at LaGuardia and National, opposed the merger. The US Department of Transportation administrative law judge (ALJ) disapproved the merger because it would increase the two carrier's shares at a number of airports, citing evidence that higher fares were associated with higher shares. DOT reversed the ALJ's decision, rejecting his reading of that evidence, market definition, and evaluation of entry barriers. The case is now pending on appeal in the US Court of Appeals.

C. Policy Issues

1. Concentration and Price

79.   Although the number of major carriers has declined in the past two years, a policy maker must be careful not to misinterpret this trend. After more than forty years of regulatory constraints, a period of consolidation is only natural. In many cases, carriers are seeking to broaden their geographic coverage in order to compete with the larger carriers and to give their passengers online service from origin to destination. All of these goals have positive benefits for consumers.

80.   The goal for future research should be to study whether, given the restructuring of the industry into large carriers with multiple hubs, a further decrease in the number of carriers will lead to a significant lessening of competition. Two new studies have looked at the question of how hubbing and traffic feed affect the relationship between concentration and price. The study by Williams, Joskow, Johnson and Hurdle (7), confirms the positive relationship for one particular geographic area. The authors studied 1985 data for all nonstop city pairs with one endpoint in St. Louis, the location of two hub carriers, TWA and Ozark. Recall that in the case of two overlapping hub carriers, successful competitive entry may require a new hub. Given the potential for high barriers, the study shows a strong effect on fares from higher concentration, especially on nonstop short haul routes where

connecting and one-stop flights are not considered good substitutes. Hurdle, Johnson, Joskow, Werden and Williams (7a), using a data set of 867 city pairs, look closely at the question of potential entry in airline markets. They find that concentration does matter if either economies of scale or economies of scope pose a significant entry barrier. These studies suggests that there continues to be a role for antitrust to ensure that air carriers do not acquire market power through consolidation.

2. Market Definition

81.   Also at issue, is the question of whether or not carriers actually compete in a nationwide market rather than on individual city pairs alone. Most studies properly focus on city pairs. However, recent anecdotal evidence indicates that carriers set fares on a nationwide basis. In some cases, higher across-the-board fares are set and then abandoned if it becomes clear that the other carriers are not going to follow. With only a small set of carriers it may be easier for them to collude on fares in all markets. This would only be true of course, if there are substantial barriers in all city-pair markets or if entry is successful only on a large scale.

82.   The question of scale of entry is becoming increasingly important. As discussed in part one, early studies estimated that carriers would begin to exhibit constant returns to scale beyond a small firm size. Yet, there is a continuing race among carriers for merger partners that will provide them with nationwide geographic coverage. There are three demand side factors that may be driving many of the acquisitions:

a) The proliferation of frequent flyer bonus programs. Travelers tend to favour large airlines over smaller carriers, because bonus awards are easier to earn if the carrier covers more potential locations. To match this capability an entrant will either have to enter at a sufficient scale or offer an award with significantly fewer flights in order to attract passengers;

b) Quality of service. There may be a perception among passegers that larger carriers provide better service because they are able to carry passengers from any origin to any destination with at most one change of plane at a hub;

c) Computer reservation systems. Although not explicitly a scale issue, it appears that carriers are seeking partnerships with carriers that own CRS systems. In part, carriers without CRSs may be trying, via merger with CRS-owing airlines, to overcome the disadvantages they perceive to have suffered from biased CRS systems. CRS systems also allow carriers to better optimize their fare menu in order to maximize total revenue.

II. AIRPORT ACCESS

A. Immunity for Airline Scheduling

83.   One of the consequences of unfettered entry has been the increased usage of limited airport resources. This, along with the expansion of hub and spoke systems, may have led to substantial increases in travel delays. According to the Department of Transportation there were 417,000 flight delays in 1986, an average of 1,144 flights every day (8). At Atlanta's Hartsfield International there are two 15 minute periods with 70 scheduled takeoffs and landings. Delay problems became so acute, that by March of 1987, DOT decided to grant the carriers antitrust immunity, allowing them to voluntarily coordinate changes in flight schedules at five of the most crowded airports (9)

84.   Antitrust immunity is, at best, a short run solution, however. One of the major avenues of competition in the airline industry is scheduling. This is particularly true in rush hour periods when the bulk of passengers are time-sensitive business travellers. Carriers have the incentive to schedule as many flights as possible at several focal points during the day. For example, a core of business travellers will be most attracted to flights that depart at 8:00 a.m. and 5:00 p.m., the two hours that define the limits of the business day. In competing for business travellers, carriers will cluster flights around these and other important hours (10).

85.   The ostensible reason for legalised collusion is that although flight schedule competition may be individually rational for each carrier, it may be beneficial to reduce it collectively. No carrier would be willing to move away from an 8:00 a.m. takeoff time by itself, because it would lose a significant number of pasengers. With a high external cost in terms of delay, however, a carrier might be willing to shift to 7:50 or 8:10 if it knew other carriers were shifting as well. Of course, any such agreement could be highly unstable. As soon as the agreements expired, schedules would naturally gravitate back to their old positions.

86.   Furthermore, any benefits from reduced delay must be balanced against the potential for anticompetitive behaviour arising from agreements that allow carriers to allocate the scarce landing times among themselves. As an alternative, the number of allowable operations could be restricted, while giving all carriers the property rights in the takeoff or landing times, with the authority to sell the right at any time. Such restrictions, known as slots, represent a possible solution to the airport congestion problem. Section B below presents an economic analysis of slots and how they work in practice. Following this, section C provides a brief discussion of how slot restrictions can act as entry barriers, with reduced competition as the unintended outcome.

B. Airport Slots

87.   The failure to grant property rights to landing times, or at least to price the landing times according to their true value will result in excessive use of a fixed resource. When deciding to serve an airport on a city pair, an airline will compare the expected revenue generated by that flight with its costs of serving the particular route. If the demand for airport access by

126

carriers is very high, that additional flight imposes costs on other carriers as well. Many of those costs can be attributed to increased safety risk and increased delay. In the process of making its decisions, however, each carrier fails to account for these external costs. As a result, there will be an excessive and inefficient level of airport usage. Because of the externality, the airport authority must restrict the number of operations below the level generated by the market. Creating a buy/sell market in a fixed number of takeoff and landing slots will insure that the scarce resource is allocated properly.

88.   There are four airports in the United States that are subject to federal regulation of takeoffs and landings -- LaGuardia and JFK in New York, O'Hare in Chicago, and National in Washington, D.C. At each of these airports there is now a fixed number of allowable landing and takeoff slots per hour. When capacity controls were originally instituted in 1968, the takeoff and landing rights were given to those carriers who already had access to the airports. The Federal Aviation Administration acted as a clearing-house for trading of slots and used its powers to force transfers of slots to new entrants.

89.   In April, 1986, the system of FAA control over slot trades was abandoned in favour of a system in which carriers could buy or sell slots on the open market. By granting saleable licences in flight times, it was felt that the slots would trade to those carriers for use on those routes that had the highest value in use. The result would be an efficient allocation of a scarce resource.

C. Airport Access and Barriers to Entry

90.   That slots might act as an impediment to entry and a hindrance to competitive performance became an issue in the merger between Texas Air and Eastern. The following example illustrates, in a general context, why the existence of slots could make entry more difficult, even when slots can be bought and sold (11).

91.   Consider a proposed merger between two carriers serving a common city pair with one endpoint at a slot-controlled aiport. Assume that there are no other apparent barriers to entry. Also assume, initially, that all slots have the same value to all carriers. Recall that a slot represents a cost to all carriers just like any other input. Any attempt by the merged entity to raise price will result in a higher than competitive return to the slot. Thus, it would be worthwhile for another carrier to shift the use of one of its slots into this market; or for a carrier not serving the airport to purchase a slot and use it in competition with the merged carrier. It appears, then, that the need for slots should not deter a carrier from disciplining anticompetitive behaviour.

92.   Even in the simple case in which slots have a common value there can be problems, though. Those carriers who might discipline the market either by shifting or buying slots, forego the return on the slot or the funds used to buy the slot. If the entry fails, it could always sell the slot, but the foregone return represents a sunk cost. The existence of even the slightest sunk costs violates the assumptions of the contestability hypothesis. It is

not at all certain that the results of this theory carry through when sunk costs are low, but positive. If the contestability hypothesis fails, then even in this simple case, the incumbent carrier could excercise market power without fear of entry.

93.   When slots take on different values across carriers the analysis becomes more complicated. For example, many of the slots may be allocated to particular uses such as feeders to hubs or to certain important times of the day like rush hour. Carriers will attribute a high value to the slots, thus making them reluctant to use them in the market in question unless the profit opportunity is very high. Thus, it is possible that the merged carrier could raise price significantly without inducing entry (12). When analyzing the merger it could be extremely difficult, if not impossible, to determine how many slots are on the margin between their current uses and a use in the affected market after a price increase.

94.   Depending on which carriers are merging and on what route, the analysis could be complicated even further. For example, if an extensive pattern of service is needed to mount an effective level of competitive entry, the transactions costs of negotiating for the needed slots and the time involved might prevent the entry. This would be especially true if a use-or-lose rule were in effect, forcing carriers to run uneconomic flights while the package is being arranged.

D. Summary

95.   Without doubt the inability to expand airport capacity and the number of airport controllers, in the short run, will necessitate some type of capacity restrictions. We should be wary, however, of regulations requiring that an omniscient policy maker determine a priori who will have rights to the scarce resources. Rather, capacity restrictions should be instituted with an eye toward allowing the price mechanism to determine the best outcome, while always remaining sensitive to the danger of mergers in highly concentrated markets with significant airport access constraints.

NOTES AND REFERENCES

1.   Moore, T., "US Airline Deregulation: Its Effects on Passengers, Capital and Labor", Journal of Law and Economics, April 1986, pp. 1-29.

2.   Morrison, S. and Winston, C., The Economic Effects of Airline Deregulation, Washington, D.C.: Brookings Institution.

3.   The cases discussed are limited to those where the carriers were direct competitors. Other mergers were primarily extensions of geographic area, with little or no overlap. For example, Delta and Western Airlines served distinct areas of the United States. Their consolidation in 1987 created a carrier with nationwide coverage.

4.   Southwest Airlines (a small hub carrier at St. Louis) received a guarantee of five gates in a settlement during the proceeding.

5.   Part II gives a more detailed analysis of slots and airport access.

6.   Airport access constraints due to noise restrictions was also important in DOT's analysis of American Airlines' acquisition of Air Cal.

7.   Williams, M., Joskow, A., Johnson, R., and Hurdle, G., "Explaining and Predicting Airline Yields With Nonparametric Regression Trees", Economics Letters, forthcoming. Economic Analysis Group Discussion Paper, EAG 87-1.

7a.   Hurdle, G., Johnson, R., Joskow, A., Werden, G. and Williams, M. "Concentration, Potential Entry and Performance in the Airline Industry," paper presented at the Southern Economics Association meetings, Washington D.C., November 1987.

8.   Department of Transportation. Final Order Granting Discussion Authority. Order 87-3-39 (March 1987).

9.   They were Atlanta, Chicago-O'Hare, Dallas-Fort Worth, Philadelphia, and Newark.

10.   Other causes include hubbing, which requires carriers to schedule flights with close connecting times. Also, it has been alleged that carriers bunch their schedules to improve their poistion on airline computer reservation screens. The latter allegations are currently being investigated at the Department of Transportation.

11. Before 1986, a new carrier could enter only after a complex bargaining process with the FAA. For example, New York Air's entry into the shuttle market was only allowed because of the FAA's mandate to aid new competition after the Deregulation Act of 1978. Clearly, a slot system without saleable licences will impose greater entry barriers than one with saleable licences.

12. Strictly speaking, the requirement is that inframarginal slot values be much higher than marginal values. The potential merger may affect enough routes so that inframarginal slots must be used.

A N N E X   I I I

THE IMPACT OF PARTIAL DEREGULATION IN THE UNITED KINGDOM DOMESTIC AIR TRANSPORT MARKET

Mr. Fod BARNES
National Consumer Council (UK)

BACKGROUND

1.   The UK domestic market has never been run as a strict state monopoly. Since the end of World War II private airlines have flown some domestic scheduled services. However, although the UK domestic sector may have had a multiplicity of airlines the idea that they might compete with each other for the same passengers is relatively new and by no means fully developed even now.

2.   Most of the major developments in relation to competition that have taken place within UK domestic regulation have occurred within the last 10 years. This paper, therefore, concentrates on the period 1976-1986 with comments on some recent developments where data is available.

LEGAL FRAMEWORK

3.   The regulatory body for the UK domestic industry is the Civil Aviation Authority (CAA). It was set up by the Civil Aviation Act of 1971 and, in relation to economic regulation, was charged with:

"(a) To secure that British airlines provide air transport services which satisfy all substantial categories of public demand (so far as British airlines may reasonably be expected to provide such services) at the lowest charges consistent with a high standard of safety in operating the services and an economic return to efficient operators on the sums invested in providing the services and with securing the sound development of the civil air transport industry of the United Kingdom;"

In addition, it had to secure that at least one major independent British airline had opportunities to participate in providing such air transport. Only subject to these two conditions was the CAA to "further the reasonable interests of users of air transport services" (2).

4.   The CAA was to discharge its duty in relation to the licencing airlines to fly particular routes following the above criteria and subject to guidance, in writing, from the Secretary of State (3). In addition, Section 22 of the Act laid down criteria that airlines had to meet, in respect of ownership and financial fitness, in order to be granted an air transport licence and Section 24 gives the Secretary of State powers to make some decisions of the CAA appealable.

5.   This Act produced a regulatory framework where the CAA's role as regards licencing competitive services was effectively determined by the policy guidance from the Secretary of State. An additional point is that although the CAA had to grant licences with regard to obtaining an economic return for efficient operators the reverse is not true -- the CAA was not obliged to revoke a licence if the carrier became inefficient. The first Guidance for the CAA was published in 1972 (4). This was revised in 1976 (5).

6.   Although neither document is particularly pro-competition the latter is considerably more restrictive in tone. The 1976 Guidance instructed the CAA to licence competing services "only if it is satisfied that", whereas the 1972 Guidance said the CAA "should licence ..... (competing services) wherever it is satisfied that ...."(6).

7.   The 1976 criteria to be used for licencing scheduled domestic services included the provisions that:

a) The scale and character of the operation of the airline(s) are within their skills and resources;

b) Efficient airlines should have the opportunity to operate profitably;

c) The entry of additional airlines should not cause undue fragmentation of effort;

d) A competing airline would only be allowed to operate if there was sufficient traffic for both airlines to operate profitably, and choice and standard of service would improve (7).

8.   The 1976 Guidance also required the CAA to publish any additional criteria it would take into account when licencing domestic (and international short-haul) scheduled services. In March 1976 the CAA published the first of these (8). In addition to the criteria outlined in the previous paragraph the CAA would not normally licence a new service unless the airline "can reasonably expect as a minimum to cover direct operating costs in the first full year of operation", and to be fully profitable within three years. New services must not increase the fares of existing services (9).

9.   Where a new service would compete directly or indirectly with an existing service, it would not be licensed if it threatened the profitability of that service (assuming the airline is efficient). In addition a new service that threatened diversion of traffic from a "hub" (eg. Birmingham or Manchester) airport would not be licensed unless the existing service operated profitably at a minimum frequency of two round trips per week day. Direct competition between city pairs would only be authorised "where a choice of airports is thus provided and the benefits to the public are clearly identifiable" (10).

10.   Thus in 1976 competition between airlines was not seen as having any intrinsic benefit, and would only be allowed if it could be demonstrated that there would be some other, fairly narrowly defined, benefit(s).

11.   In 1979 the Government proposed (and subsequently carried out) the amendment of the Civil Aviation Act 1971 to remove the provision whereby the Secretary of State gives guidance to the CAA. The amendment of the Act also made it a requirement of the CAA to publish, from time to time, a statement of its policies on licensing and elaborated the requirement of the CAA to carry out its duties to "further the reasonable interests of the users of air transport services" to that of equal status with its duty to British Airlines as quoted in paragraph 3 above. In addition, the amendment requires that the CAA "have regard in particular to any benefits which may arise from enabling two or more airlines to provide the services in question". This resulted in

the CAA issuing a further statement on Air Transport Licencing Policies (11). This new statement is interesting in that the objectives of CAA policy were shifted.

> "The Authority has tried to build up over the last few years a policy framework within which individual decisions may stand coherently. These policies are directed towards the sound development of a highly regulated industry in the service of the users of air transport. To a large extent, in carrying out these policies, the Authority has to provide regulatory substitutes for absent or weakened market forces." (12)

12. For the first time, the CAA introduced the explicit threat of substitution, even if the cards were still stacked in the existing operator's favour.

> "Where these constraints (on direct competition) apply, competition will take the form of the threat of substitution. The Authority will require a powerful case to be made before transferring to another operator a route which the incumbent operator is serving well and profitably."(13).

13. At the time these criteria were issued the CAA was in the middle of a public consultation on domestic regulatory policy (14). This consultation, and a more general consultation on licensing policy, led to the publication of new Statement of Policies on Air Transport Licencing in April 1981 (15).

14. The 1981 Statement of Policies reflected the increasingly pro-competitive stance being taken by the CAA. The CAA would "favour" competing services that would better satisfy the consumer in terms of:

> " (i) Wider choice (including, for example, choice of airport, seat availability, range of products); or
>
> (ii) Greater carrier efficiency which may be reflected in lower tariffs and improved standards of service; or
>
> (iii) The stimulation of innovation on the part of incumbent carriers." (16)

15. However, the favourable regard with which licences for competing services were now to be viewed was also tempered by the reservation that the CAA "will wish first to satisfy itself that the volume and type of traffic currently on the route and increased carryings which might reasonably be expected as a result of the competitive stimulus will be likely to allow a reasonable prospect of profitable operation by efficient British airlines" (17).

16. And, just as importantly:

> "Where competition is precluded or not attainable on acceptable terms the Authority must consider the possibility of substituting a new carrier for an incumbent on a route as a means of ensuring that users' interests are safeguarded. The Authority will not lightly revoke a licence which is currently being used." (18)

17.   In 1983 the CAA embarked on a consultation exercise on Airline Competition Policy, which resulted in an interim report (19) and final report in July 1984 (20). Both reports favoured more competition. The final report also modified the 1981 Statement of Policies on Air Transport Licencing, proposing the introduction of an "area licence", which would licence a carrier to fly any domestic route (except for some specified routes). In addition, the CAA would replace the system of detailed fare approval by one of fare filing (21) (see below for more details on the changes in fare regulations).

18.   A new Statement of Policies on Air Transport Licencing was issued in January 1985, which confirmed the proposal to change the domestic fare approval system, and a two year experiment in allowing free access to some domestic routes (22). However, in the event, the proposal to allow free access to some domestic routes was dropped in July 1985 (23), while the proposal on tariff filing was approved (24) and came into effect in September 1985. This new statement also slightly reduced the economic barriers to licensing competing services by stipulating that "loss of profit to an incumbent carrier need not in itself constitute a bar to the licensing of a competing service". However, within the time frame of this paper (1976-1986) these new provisions will not have had much of an impact.

FARES

19.   The regulatory objectives of the fare approval process has also evolved over the period 1976 to 1986. The 1976 Guidance stated:

"The Authority should seek to secure tariff provisions and associated conditions that are rational, simple and enforceable. As a guiding principle for the longer term, each charge should be related to costs at a level which will yield sufficient revenue to cover the costs of efficient operators, including an adequate return on capital" (25).

20.   By 1981 the CAA had prefaced its objectives on pricing with "where possible the Authority will allow market forces to set or influence the level of fares and rates for air transport" (26). However, the criteria to be used for approving a fare remained largely the same. The 1985 Statement of Policies on Air Transport Licensing followed the line of the 1981 one, and is still in force (27). The change in the tariff filing method in September 1985 did not alter these objectives.

21.   In practice airlines have filed for approval to vary existing fares, and regulatory intervention has concentrated on the justification, or otherwise, of that change. To a certain extent this has been true, even when an approval for a new fare type on a route is being sought.

22.   In addition, although the objectives of fare approval were to set fares with reference to an efficient airline, in practice this has usually meant that fares are set with reference to the operations of the filing airline, efficient or otherwise.

23.   The combination of lack of direct competition between airlines, the reluctance of the CAA to substitute one airline for another on a particular route and a fare approval mechanism which, in the end, has to assume the filing airline is efficient has produced a regulatory structure which is not particularly robust in relation to price. In addition, where airlines are in competition with each other there is an implicit right for each airline to be able to match each others' fares as, by definition, the fare is approved for "an efficient airline". This has serious implications when the competing airlines are of significantly different sizes and financial strengths.

CAPACITY

24.   Capacity is not formally regulated. To fly a particular route airlines need a route licence and fare approval, and although both applications may use a projected output (usually frequency and aircraft type) airlines are free to alter the capacity they actually mount.

25.   However, some routes to and from Heathrow may experience a type of frequency control in so far as the airline is unable to gain access to useable take-off and landing slots.

THE PRACTICAL EXTENT OF DIRECT AND INDIRECT COMPETITION

26.   Even in 1986 the licencing of new competitive services is the exception, rather than the rule. Most UK domestic routes are operated by only one carrier. Of the over 180 scheduled routes being flown in May 1986 only 27 are flown by two or more airlines. A further three routes face indirect competition from different London airports (28). Table 1 lists these routes with their annual passenger traffic. (In terms of passenger numbers the non monopoly routes are more important, carrying about 75 per cent of all passengers.)

27.   In 1981 there were 12 routes with more than one airline operating, and a further two routes with indirect competition from different London airports. In 1976 the figures were eight and two respectively (29). (In 1976 there were no price differentials -- see below.)

28.   Although the number of routes with direct (potential) competition between airlines has increased a number of them are rather thin, and could be expected to be flown co-operatively rather than competitively.

29.   As would be expected, competition has been most visible and vigorous on the major trunk routes out of London (i.e. London to Belfast, Manchester, Glasgow and Edinburgh). However, because these routes use the London airports and airlines would prefer to use Heathrow, they are partially protected from the threat of new entry by the capacity constraints on Heathrow. There is an effective presumption against new airlines and new routes using Heathrow for domestic purposes.

30.   As has been described above up to about 1982 there was no effective, direct competition between airlines. Regulation effectively protected the incumbent airline from either substitution or the licencing of a direct competitor. Indirect competition was possible, but only if there would be no undue effect on the existing route. In October 1982, on appeal to the Secretary of State, the first really serious directly competitive licence was issued. British Midland were licensed on the Heathrow-Glasgow route in competition with British Airways. Direct competition subsequently emerged on the routes out of Heathrow to Edinburgh (1983), Belfast (1984) and Manchester (1985) (30).

Table 1

ROUTES WITH COMPETITION IN 1986
(* routes indirect competition)

**Annual passenger traffic 1986, thousands
(includes domestic charter passengers)**

Route	
Aberdeen to Edinburgh	14.6
Glasgow	35.2
London *	425.1
Manchester	39.8
Newcastle	9.4
Belfast to Birmingham	98.2
Blackpool	23.8
Glasgow	66.2
Isle of Man	27.1
London	978.2
Manchester	142.3
Birmingham to London *	95.4
Blackpool to Isle of Man	35.2
Edinburgh to Jersey	8.6 (1)
Kirkwall	6.7
Lerwick	1.6
London	1086.7
Exeter to Jersey	48.6 (1)
Glasgow to Inverness	17.1
London	1102.5
Manchester	67.8
Guernsey to Jersey	n.a
London *	604.7 (1)
Inverness to Kirkwall	7.2
Jersey to London	604.7 (1)
Manchester	104.7 (1)
London to Manchester	876.2
Newcastle	324.7
Norwich	16.6
Teeside	148.8

1.   Includes all Channel Island traffic.

Source: CAA Annual Statistics (1986), ABC World Airways Guide (May 1986)

EFFECT ON AIRLINE OUTPUT: FARES

31.   The following analysis of fares is based on data taken mainly from the ABC Guide and the UK DAT CAP 397/CAA DOC 295. A 20 per cent sample of all the routes being flown in all of the three years 1976, 1981 and 1986 was used as the basis for the comparisons with the sub-groups of routes, namely:

-- High frequency routes (more than 10 flights per day in 1986);

-- Medium frequency routes (5-9 flights per day in 1986);

-- Low frequency routes flown by one airline (3-4 flights per day in 1986).

In addition, the routes used by the CAA in their report "Competition on the main domestic trunk routes" are analysed.

32.   Table 2 gives the changes in the one-way economy fare for all these sub groups, and compares that with average results for the 20 per cent sample. (In all cases where the average results of the sample are being used the full Table for these routes will be given in Annex 1, using the same Table number with the suffix A.)

Table 2

ECONOMY FARES
HIGH FREQUENCY ROUTES WITH DIRECT COMPETITION

	1976 £	1981 £	% Change 76-81	1986	% Change 81-86	% Change 76-86
Belfast London	25.00	44.00	76	63.66	45	155
Edinburgh London	24.00	55.00	129	68.33	24	184
Glasgow London	24.00	55.00	129	68.33	24	184
Jersey London	17.90	38.83	117	49.42	27	176
London Manchester	18.20	39.00	114	53.66	38	195
AVERAGE			113		32	179
CAA COMPARISON ROUTES						
Aberdeen London	31.90	57.00	79	77.00	35	141
IOM London	20.20	41.75	107	65.00	56	221
Liverpool London	18.20	38.00	109	56.00	47	208
London Newcastle	21.40	46.00	115	63.00	37	194
AVERAGE			103		44	191

Table 2 (Cont'd)

	1976 £	1981 £	% Change 76-81	1986	% Change 81-86	% Change 76-86
MEDIUM FREQUENCY ROUTES IN 1986 (5-9 FLIGHTS A DAY)						
Aberdeen Edinburgh	11.30	29.50	161	40.00	36	254
Aberdeen Glasgow	12.80	35.00	173	50.50	44	294
Aberdeen London	31.90	57.00	79	77.00	35	141
Aberdeen Manchester	30.20	66.00	118	86.50	31	186
Belfast Birmingham	21.90	45.50	108	62.00	36	183
Belfast Glasgow	12.80	32.50	153	47.66	46	272
Belfast Manchester	17.30	40.00	131	55.75	39	222
Birmingham London	12.60	29.75	136	50.00	68	296
IOM Liverpool	12.30	29.00	136	42.00	45	241
Leeds London	19.20	38.00	98	62.50	64	225
Liverpool London	18.20	38.00	109	56.00	47	208
London Newcastle	21.40	46.00	115	63.00	37	194
London Teeside	18.90	45.00	138	65.50	46	247
Southampton Jersey	13.50	28.50	111	38.00	33	181
AVERAGE			126		43	225
SINGLE OPERATOR ROUTES, 3-4 DAILY FREQUENCY						
NON BA OPERATED IN 1986						
Belfast Leeds	18.90	43.50	130	55.00	26	191
Belfast Liverpool	16.80	36.00	114	47.00	31	180
Bournemouth Jersey	13.30	28.50	114	37.50	32	182
Edinburgh Manchester	14.50	41.00	183	55.50	35	283
IOM Manchester	13.60	29.00	113	44.00	52	224
IOM London	20.20	41.75	107	65.00	56	222
AVERAGE			127		39	214
BA OPERATED						
Aberdeen Birmingham	32.90	67.00	104	84.00	25	155
Aberdeen Lerwick	22.80	49.50	117	70.00	41	207
Birmingham Edinburgh	24.90	55.50	123	72.00	30	189
Glasgow Lerwick	32.20	77.50	141	107.00	38	232
AVERAGE			121		33	196
20% SAMPLE						
Average			111		44	196
Range			30-157		25-77	78-272
Inter-quartile range			101-130		32-53	169-226

Note: Where airline specific price differences exist a simple mean is used for this table.

Table 3

FARES INDEXED 1976 = 100, DEFLATED BY RPI

	1976	1981	1986
HIGH DENSITY ROUTES WITH DIRECT COMPETITION			
Belfast London	100	93	103
Edinburgh London	100	122	115
Glasgow London	100	122	115
Jersey London	100	115	112
London Manchester	100	114	120
AVERAGE		113	113
CAA COMPARISON ROUTES			
Aberdeen London	100	95	98
IOM London	100	110	130
Liverpool London	100	111	125
London Newcastle	100	114	119
AVERAGE		108	118
MEDIUM FREQUENCY ROUTES IN 1986 (5-9 FLIGHTS A DAY)			
Aberdeen Edinburgh	100	139	145
Aberdeen Glasgow	100	145	160
Aberdeen London	100	95	98
Aberdeen Manchester	100	116	116
Belfast Birmingham	100	110	115
Belfast Glasgow	100	135	151
Belfast Manchester	100	123	131
Birmingham London	100	126	161
IOM Liverpool	100	126	138
Leeds London	100	105	132
Liverpool London	100	111	125
London Newcastle	100	114	119
London Teeside	100	127	141
Southampton Jersey	100	112	114
AVERAGE		120	132

Table 3 (Cont'd)

	1976	1981	1986
SINGLE OPERATOR ROUTES, 3–4 DAILY FREQUENCY			
NON BA OPERATED IN 1986			
Belfast Leeds	100	122	118
Belfast Liverpool	100	114	114
Bournemouth Jersey	100	114	114
Edinburgh Manchester	100	151	155
IOM Manchester	100	113	131
IOM London	100	110	131
AVERAGE	100	121	127
BA OPERATED in 1986			
Aberdeen Birmingham	100	109	103
Aberdeen Lerwick	100	116	125
Birmingham Edinburgh	100	119	117
Glasgow Lerwick	100	128	135
AVERAGE	100	118	120
20% SAMPLE			
Average	100	112	120
Range	–	69–137	72–151
Inter-quartile range	–	107–122	109–132

33.   Table 3 presents the same information in index form, (1976=100), deflated by the Retail Price Index.

34.   The results for the high frequency routes are similar to to the 20 per cent sample. If anything price rises on these routes are slightly below the average for the sample. However, considering that in the period covered there has been vigorous competition on these routes, and that on a number of occasions there have been significant price differentials between the different airlines operating on the same route, a result that is only just below average is not particularly significant.

35.   The results for the medium frequency routes is more interesting. These tend to show higher than average increases over the ten years 1976–86, with most of the above average price increases taking place in the first half of the period (1976–81).

36.   All the medium frequency routes except Jersey to Southampton and Isle
of Man to Liverpool were flown by two or more airlines in 1986, and over half
of the routes gained a competitor in the second five year period (1981-86). In
the first five years three routes gained competitors and two routes lost them.
See Table 4.

Table 4

NUMBER OF OPERATORS

	1976	1981	1986
HIGH DENSITY ROUTES WITH DIRECT COMPETITION			
Belfast London	2	2	3
Edinburgh London	2	2	3
Glasgow London	2	2	3
Jersey London	3	3	6
London Manchester	2	2	3
CAA COMPARISON ROUTES			
Aberdeen London	1	2	2
IOM London	1	2	1
Liverpool London	1	1	2
London Newcastle	2	1	2

MEDIUM FREQUENCY ROUTES IN 1986 (5-9 FLIGHTS A DAY)

Number of airlines on route, direct and indirect competition

	1976	1981	1986
Aberdeen Edinburgh	3	3	3
Aberdeen Glasgow	1	2	2
Aberdeen London	1	2	2
Aberdeen Manchester	1	1	2
Belfast Birmingham	1	1	2
Belfast Glasgow	1	1	3
Belfast Manchester	1	1	2
Birmingham London	2	2	2
IOM Liverpool	1	1	1
Leeds London	1	2	2
Liverpool London	1	1	2
London Newcastle	2	1	2
London Teeside	1	1	2
Southampton Jersey	2	1	1

37.   The medium frequency routes recording the two lowest increases in the 1976-81 period both gained competitors, although the third route gaining a competitor, (Aberdeen to Glasgow), showed the largest increase. (A possible explanation for this is that the airline entering the Aberdeen to Glasgow route was already competing with the other airlines on that route on the route Aberdeen to Edinburgh.) In the second period (1981-86) the lowest fare increase (Aberdeen to Manchester) was recorded on a route gaining competition, and the two routes showing the highest fare increases (Birmingham to London and Leeds to London) saw no change in competition. (In addition, on these two routes the competing airlines use different London airports.)

38.   Over the ten year period the route London to Birmingham showed the largest price rise, and saw no change in the level of competition. Aberdeen to Glasgow came next, with a change in the first period (but see above), followed by Belfast to Glasgow (additional airline in 1981-86, with an average price rise, no change in competition in 1976-81, with the third largest increase). Aberdeen to Edinburgh, the other route with no change in the level of competition, had the fourth highest price rise. (Jersey to Southampton, which lost competition, went against this trend, showing a below average price increase.)

39.   Analysis of the results for the high frequency routes shows a similar pattern. In the first period (1976-81) there is no change in the competitive environment and price increases are about average. In the second period (1981-86), when an additional carrier and direct competition (ie using the same London airport) are introduced, the average price increase is below (23 per cent below) the sample average. Individually, all routes show average or below average price rises, with three out of the five being below the lower quartile of the sample.

40.   However, the level of economy fares is only half the picture in terms of the price the passengers actually pay. Some passengers travel on discount tickets, so the average price paid by travellers is less than the economy fare. Unfortunately, the data on how many passengers travel on discount tickets, and which discount tickets, is not available to the public, as the airlines will not release it. However, it is possible to look at some proxies for this data, which can give some indication of the way the market is changing.

41.   Table 5 shows the price of the lowest discount ticket available to the public for travel only (i.e. not the air fare part of an inclusive tour ticket) as of the 1st May for 1976, 1981 and 1986, for travel on, or around the 1st May (i.e. seasonal discount tickets are only counted if they include travel in May). The prices are expressed as a percentage of the price of the economy ticket.

145

Table 5

DISCOUNT FARES: LOWEST DISCOUNT FARE AS A PERCENTAGE OF ECONOMY FARE

	1976	1981	1986
HIGH DENSITY ROUTES WITH DIRECT COMPETITION			
Belfast London	64	64	35
Edinburgh London	58	45	50
Glasgow London	58	45	50
Jersey London	100	64	60
London Manchester	100	51	51
AVERAGE (all fares)	76	54	49
Average (disc. fares only)	60	54	49
CAA COMPARISON ROUTES			
Aberdeen London	62	49	29
IOM London	88	57	68
Liverpool London	71	66	64
London Newcastle	65	46	52
AVERAGE (all fares)	72	55	53
MEDIUM FREQUENCY ROUTES IN 1986 (5-9 FLIGHTS A DAY)			
Aberdeen Edinburgh	100	51	50
Aberdeen Glasgow	100	51	56
Aberdeen London	62	49	29
Aberdeen Manchester	64	50	31
Belfast Birmingham	100	75	48
Belfast Glasgow	100	67	59
Belfast Manchester	100	71	43
Birmingham London	100	64	56
IOM Liverpool	83	34	47
Leeds London	100	47	43
Liverpool London	71	66	64

Table 5 (Cont'd)

	1976	1981	1986
SINGLE OPERATOR ROUTES, 3-4 DAILY FREQUENCY			
NON BA OPERATED IN 1986			
Belfast Leeds	100	51	76
Belfast Liverpool	100	69	79
Bournemouth Jersey	61	70	73
Edinburgh Manchester	66	50	93
IOM Manchester	100	50	81
IOM London	100	57	68
AVERAGE (all fares)	88	58	78
Average (disc. fares only)	64	58	78
BA OPERATED			
Aberdeen Birmingham	100	49	38
Aberdeen Lerwick	100	67	54
Birmingham Edinburgh	50	50	37
Glasgow Lerwick	100	63	57
AVERAGE (all fares)	88	57	47
20 % SAMPLE			
Average (all fares)	89	62	66
Range	61-100	32-100	34-100
Inter-quartile range	89-100	51-70	52-77
Average (disc. fares only)	69	60	62
Range	61-89	32-81	34-83
Inter-quartile range	62-84	50-70	52-73

42.   Table 6 shows the number of different types of discount ticket available on each route, and Table 7 gives the same results for the medium and high frequency routes averaged for each airline on the route, (i.e. if on a particular route there are eight different discount tickets available and two airlines flying Table 6 shows eight and Table 7 shows four).

Table 6

NUMBER OF DIFFERENT TYPES OF DISCOUNT TICKETS AVAILABLE PER ROUTE

	1976	1981	1986
HIGH DENSITY ROUTES WITH DIRECT COMPETITION			
Belfast London	3	6	15
Edinburgh London	3	7	16
Glasgow London	3	7	15
Jersey London	0	8	12
London Manchester	0	6	9
AVERAGE	1.8	6.8	13.4
CAA COMPARISON ROUTES			
Aberdeen London	1	6	10
IOM London	0	7	3
Liverpool London	1	3	3
London Newcastle	2	5	8
AVERAGE	1.3	5.3	6
MEDIUM FREQUENCY ROUTES IN 1986 (5–9 FLIGHTS A DAY)			
Aberdeen Edinburgh	0	7	9
Aberdeen Glasgow	0	4	5
Aberdeen London	1	6	10
Aberdeen Manchester	1	1	6
Belfast Birmingham	0	1	4
Belfast Glasgow	0	2	6
Belfast Manchester	0	1	7
Birmingham London	0	3	4
IOM Liverpool	1	4	1
Leeds London	0	6	8
Liverpool London	1	3	3
London Newcastle	2	5	8
London Teeside	1	3	8
Southampton Jersey	0	5	3
AVERAGE	0.5	3.6	5.4

Table 6 (Cont'd)

	1976	1981	1986

SINGLE OPERATOR ROUTES IN 1986, 3-4 DAILY FREQUENCY

NON BA OPERATED IN 1986

	1976	1981	1986
Belfast Leeds	0	4	2
Belfast Liverpool	0	2	3
Bournemouth Jersey	1	3	7
Edinburgh Manchester	1	2	1
IOM Manchester	0	4	1
IOM London	0	7	3
AVERAGE	0.3	3.7	2.8

BA OPERATED

	1976	1981	1986
Aberdeen Birmingham	0	1	4
Aberdeen Lerwick	0	1	3
Birmingham Edinburgh	1	1	4
Glasgow Lerwick	0	1	3
AVERAGE	0.3	1	3.5

Table 7

NUMBER OF DIFFERENT TYPES OF DISCOUNT TICKETS AVAILABLE PER ROUTE, PER AIRLINE (AVERAGE)

	1976	1981	1986
HIGH DENSITY ROUTES WITH DIRECT COMPETITION			
Belfast London	1.5	3	5
Edinburgh London	1.5	3.5	5.3
Glasgow London	1.5	3.5	5
Jersey London	0	2.7	2
London Manchester	0	3	3
AVERAGE	0.9	3.14	4.1
CAA COMPARISON ROUTES			
Aberdeen London	1	3	5
IOM London	1	3.5	3
Liverpool London	1	3	1.5
London Newcastle	1	5	4
AVERAGE	1	3.6	3.4
MEDIUM FREQUENCY ROUTES IN 1986 (5-9 FLIGHTS A DAY)			
Aberdeen Edinburgh	0	2.3	3
Aberdeen Glasgow	0	2	2.5
Aberdeen London	1	3	5
Aberdeen Manchester	1	1	3
Belfast Birmingham	0	1	2
Belfast Glasgow	0	2	2
Belfast Manchester	0	1	3.5
Birmingham London	0	1.5	2
IOM Liverpool	1	4	1
Leeds London	0	3	4
Liverpool London	1	3	1.5
London Newcastle	1	5	4
London Teeside	1	3	4
Southampton Jersey	0	5	3
AVERAGE	0.4	2.6	2.9

43.   The major development over the ten year period has been the considerable increase in the number of discount tickets available, and the increase in the level of discount for the cheapest ticket. As might be expected both the number and level of discount increase with the route frequency. The increase in number is partially explained by the increase in the number of routes with more than one airline as frequency increases. However, even when the number of ticket types available on a particular route is divided by the number of airlines flying the route (Table 7) the relationship still holds.

44.   However, the major increase in the availability of discount tickets takes place in the first time period (1976-81), rather than the second (1981-86), while the number of routes gaining competition is higher in the second period. Even so, there may be some effect of competition on the number of types of discount ticket available. See Table 8.

Table 8

CHANGES IN THE AVERAGE NUMBER OF DISCOUNT TICKETS AVAILABLE, PER ROUTE

	1976-81	1981-86	1976-86
High frequency	5	6.6	11.6
Med frequency	3.1	1.8	4.9
20% sample	1.9	0.9	2.8

CHANGES IN THE AVERAGE NUMBER OF DISCOUNT TICKETS AVAILABLE, PER AIRLINE, PER ROUTE

	1976-81	1981-86	1976-86
High frequency	2.2	1.0	3.2
Med frequency	2.2	0.3	2.5
20% sample	1.9	0.3	2.2
BA monopoly routes (1)	0.7	2.5	3.2
Non BA monopoly (1)	3.4	-0.9	2.5

1.   Routes with 3-4 daily frequency in 1986.

Source: UK DAT data, ABC World Airways Guide.

45.   From the passengers point of view, the actual availablilty of a discount ticket for a particular journey will depend on whether or not they can meet the conditions imposed. As the number of different discount ticket types goes up the chances of being able to meet the conditions for at least one ticket type increases. However, if competing airlines offer very similar discount tickets the actual choice available is really equivalent to the number that one airline offers. But, if the ticket types are different, the range of ticket types available is the sum of the two airlines offerings. In reality, the real range will be somewhere in between these two extremes, probably closer to the former rather than the latter.

151

46.   An additional, and more serious complication is that the real availability of useable discount tickets depends on the actual conditions imposed, and the capacity limitations (if any) applied by the airline. Clearly, a discount ticket that is easily available could be 'worth' more than a selection of highly restrictive tickets. Table 9 gives the number of passengers using discount tickets for the complete domestic network in 1981 and 1986. (Figures for 1976 are unavailable, although as the number of discount ticket types actually available in 1976 was small there is unlikely to have been much of this sort of traffic.)

Table 9

NUMBER OF PASSENGERS USING DISCOUNT TICKETS
(Millions)

	1981 M	1986 M	change %
Total scheduled passengers	6.04	8.08	33
Full price tickets	4.31	4.91	15
Discount tickets	1.73	3.17	83
Discount as % of total	29	39	

Source: CAA Annual Statistics.

47.   Most of the increase (79 per cent) in traffic from 1981 to 1986 was accounted for by the increase in discount travel. If discount travel had expanded at the same rate as the total market the figure for 1986 should have been 2.3 million, rather than 3.17 million. Although external factors will have had an influence on the differential growth of the full price and discount market it is also quite likely that conditions attached to the discount tickets have become easier to fulfil. The expected increase in discount passengers because of the increased availability (ie increase in the number of ticket types) may account for some of this extra increase.

48.   As was stated above the figures for the number of discount tickets sold on a route by route basis are not publicly available. It is therefore difficult to see if there are any patterns that emerge in relation to the degree of competition on particular routes.

Conclusion on fares

49.   Within the limitations of the liberalised UK domestic market there is no obvious and definite link between the number of carriers on a route and the rate of increase in economy fares. If there is a link at all it is that the actual entry of a new carrier would seem to reduce the economy fares in a one off manner. The more detail analysis of the four major domestic trunks over the shorter period of 1980–1985 done by the CAA (CAA paper 87005, 1987) supports this view (31).

50.   There does, however, seem to be a quite strong link between the number of types of discount ticket available and the frequency of operation and/or the number of carriers on a route. (For sound economic reasons high frequency routes are also likely to be flown by more than one carrier, and vice-versa.) A similar relationship exists between these types of routes and the depth of the maximum discount.

51.   This is not altogether surprising. If it is assumed that the passengers using economy tickets are not particularly price sensitive, and that the regulatory body will neither allow one airline to charge economy fares that would threaten the operation of one of the existing carriers nor stop competitors from matching a fare even if this will entail cross-subsidy, then price competition in this market is unlikely to be a rational strategy. However, price competition for the more price sensitive part of the market (the discount part) would be more rational. This is what appears to have happened.

ROUTE NETWORK AND TRAFFIC

52.   The total number of points served by the domestic scheduled network has increased over the 10 year period from 46 to 51, and the number of routes from 314 to 372 (each route counted once in each direction). The route network has become slightly more dense over the period. However, the share of the network accounted for by routes from the 15 or 5 largest airports has not changed significantly. See Table 10.

Table 10

UK DOMESTIC ROUTES, AIRPORT ACTIVITY

	1976	1981	1986
Number of points served	46	50	51
Total number of routes	314	356	372
% change		13%	4%
Average number of routes per point served	6.8	7.1	7.3
Number of routes from the 15 busiest airports (1)	176	199	210
% of Total	56%	56%	56%
Number of routes from the 5 busiest airports (1)	78	88	96
% of Total	25%	25%	26%

1. London is treated as one airport

Source: ABC Guide, May 1976, 1981, 1986. UK DAT data.

153

Table 11

UK DOMESTIC SCHEDULED TRAFFIC, AIRPORT USE

	1976	1981	1986
Total number of passengers using all UK airports (million)	13.6	14.6	19.3
% change		7%	32%
Total number of passengers using 15 busiest airports (1)	12.2	13.3	17.6
% of Total	90	91	91
% change		9%	32%
Total number of passengers using 5 busiest airports (1)	8.3	9.3	12.7
% of Total	61	64	66
% change		12%	37%

1. London is counted as one airport, figures not directly comparable with passenger uplift.

Source: CAA Annual Statistics.

Table 12

UK DOMESTIC TRAFFIC, ROUTE USE

	1976	1981	1986
Total passenger uplift (1)	6.1	6.6	9.1
% change		8%	38%
% change 1976-86		49%	

1. Includes inclusive tour passengers.

Table 12 (Cont'd)

TOTAL NUMBER OF PASSENGERS PER ANNUM. (INCLUDES CHARTER)

Million

	1976 M	1981 M	1986 M
HIGH DENSITY ROUTES WITH DIRECT COMPETITION			
Belfast London	.469	.673	.978
Edinburgh London	.677	.640	1.087
Glasgow London	.887	.756	1.103
Jersey London	.553	.404	.652
London Manchester	.456	.566	.876
TOTAL	3.044	3.039	4.696
% change		-0.1	55
CAA COMPARISON ROUTES			
Aberdeen London	.218	.393	.425
IOM London	.072	.058	.079
Liverpool London	.119	.080	.079
London Newcastle	.283	.281	.325
TOTAL	.693	.812	.878
% change		17	8
MEDIUM FREQUENCY ROUTES IN 1986 (5-9 FLIGHTS A DAY)			
Aberdeen Edinburgh	.018	.019	.015
Aberdeen Glasgow	.044	.051	.035
Aberdeen London	.218	.393	.425
Aberdeen Manchester	.005	.025	.040
Belfast Birmingham	.069	.069	.098
Belfast Glasgow	.092	.064	.077
Belfast Manchester	.124	.115	.142
Birmingham London	.099	.086	.095
IOM Liverpool	.046	.049	.107
Leeds London	.123	.095	.135
Liverpool London	.119	.080	.049
London Newcastle	.283	.281	.325
London Teeside	.122	.113	.149
Southampton Jersey	.256	.193	.245
TOTAL	1.618	1.632	1.936
% change		0.8	19

53.   Total traffic, on the other hand has grown quite considerably (see Table 12). The increase in traffic on the high frequency routes in the second period (1981-86) is quite dramatic, increasing by over 50 per cent. By contrast, the traffic on all other domestic routes grew by only 22 per cent. In the previous period, however, there was no growth overall on these routes, while the traffic in the rest of the market grew by around 16 per cent. In the first period more routes were added than in the second (increasing by 13 per cent as compared with 4 per cent).

54.   The average number of passengers per route fell from 1976 to 1981 (from about 19,400 per annum to 18,500), but rose quite sharply from 1981 to 1986 (up to 24,500 p.a.).

55.   From a regulatory point of view this is not all that surprising. In the first period airlines were either acting as monopolists on their routes, or where there was direct or indirect competition, the regulatory system allowed them (and probably encouraged them) to act as oligopolists. There was, therefore, not much incentive for existing operators try very hard to meet consumer demand. Regulation effectively protected the airlines from the threat of substitution and traffic diversion. However, even in the first period the CAA would licence new airlines to fly new routes. There was, therefore, a threat of entry in this market area.

56.   In the second period direct competition was introduced on the domestic trunks into Heathrow, and the airline entering was a serious threat to the existing carrier. On these routes at least there was an incentive for the airlines to try to meet consumer demand. It would be expected that this would increase the total number of passengers on these routes (which it did). The number of other routes gaining a second carrier was also higher in the second period than the first.

Conclusion on routes and traffic

57.   The CAA's change to a more pro-competitive regulatory stance in the period 1981-1986 has resulted in a considerable increase in the traffic carried on existing routes. Some of the growth on these routes can be explained by outside economic factors, but the change in the way the market grew between the first and second periods suggests that the type regulation imposed has also had a significant influence.

Frequency of service

58.   Traffic growth on a route can be accommodated by increases in aircraft size, or by increases in frequency of service. In addition, frequency of service can be increased (or decreased) without changes in traffic by changing the average load factor (per cent of available seats actually filled). Table 13 summarises what has happened in the UK domestic market, and Table 14 compares passenger growth with frequency change.

Table 13

FREQUENCY OF SERVICE, PER WEEK DAY

	1976	1981	1986
HIGH DENSITY ROUTES WITH DIRECT COMPETITION			
Belfast London	9	10	17
Edinburgh London	11	11	21
Glasgow London	17	14	22
Jersey London	9	7	10
London Manchester	11	11	15
AVERAGE	11.4	10.6	17
CAA COMPARISON ROUTES			
Aberdeen London	5	10	8
IOM London	4	2	3
Liverpool London	3	4	5
London Newcastle	9	7	8
AVERAGE	5.25	5.75	6
MEDIUM FREQUENCY ROUTES IN 1986 (5-9 FLIGHTS A DAY)			
Aberdeen Edinburgh	5	5	5
Aberdeen Glasgow	2	5	7
Aberdeen London	5	10	8
Aberdeen Manchester	1	1	5
Belfast Birmingham	2	2	5
Belfast Glasgow	4	3	7
Belfast Manchester	3	3	5
Birmingham London	4	7	8
IOM Liverpool	3	1	5
Leeds London	4	4	7
Liverpool London	3	4	5
London Newcastle	9	7	8
London Teeside	5	4	7
Southampton Jersey	8	5	6
AVERAGE	4.14	4.36	6.23

Table 14

PASSENGER GROWTH COMPARED TO FREQUENCY CHANGE (%)

Change in number of passengers per route compared with
change in frequency of operation

P=% change in passenger numbers
F=% change in service frequency

	1976-81		1981-86		1976-86	
	P	F	P	F	P	F
Total market (1)	-4.5	1	32	24	26	25
High frequency routes	-0.1	-7	55	60	54	49
Med. frequency routes	0.8	5	19	44	20	51

1.   The figures for frequency should be treated with caution as they are based on the 20 per cent route sample, which does not include any new routes added in the period 1976-86.

Source: ABC World Airways Guide, CAA Annual Statistics.

59.   Over the 10 year period the overall average number of passengers per plane has not altered. On the high frequency routes the average number of passengers per plane has increased slightly, but on the medium frequency routes average passenger numbers have declined (by the order of about 20 per cent).

60.   However, in terms of airline efficiency the load factor per aircraft is more important than the actual number of passengers per plane.

Table 15

AVERAGE LOAD FACTORS, UK DOMESTIC SCHEDULED SERVICES

	1976	1981	1986
Total, all airlines	60.8	63.2	60.6
British Airways	63.4	66.6	60.9
Air UK	58.4 (1)	59.9	61.9
British Caledonian	49.3	56.1	60.2
BMA	56.1	59.1	58.3
Dan Air	52.4	60.8	62.2

1. Air Anglia figure.

Source: CAA Annual Statistics (1976,1981,1986).

61.   Load factors increased in the first period, when average numbers of passengers per aircraft increased slightly, and fell in the second period when passenger numbers per aircraft fell more sharply. However, the fall in load factors is not as steep as the fall in passenger numbers per aircraft. Some of the general increase in frequency must, therefore, be accounted for by a decrease in plane size.

62.   Load factors for the four major domestic trunk routes are available for the period 1980-1985. Table 16 compares the results for these routes with the overall load factors and the relevant airline load factors.

Table 16

LOAD FACTORS ON THE DOMESTIC TRUNKS

	1981	1985
Total, all airlines	63.2	62.3
British Airways, all	66.6	63.7
Lon. to Belfast	73.3	63.5
Edinburgh	67.9	65.3
Glasgow	66.9	64.8
Manchester	60.8	65.4
British Caledonian, all	56.1	60.6
Lon. to Edinburgh	62.5	60.1
Glasgow	59.3	62.2
Manchester	50.1	53.2
British Midland, all	59.1	59.5
Lon. to Belfast	65.6	56.5
Edinburgh	-	57.8
Glasgow	-	57.1
Dan Air, all	60.8	60.0
Lon. to Belfast	-	58.3
Manchester	-	19.7

Source: CAA Annual Statistics, and CAA Paper 87005.

63.   British Airways' load factor performance on the domestic trunks has generally been better than both the average load factor for the total market and its own average load factor. The introduction of direct competition on these routes does not seem to have much effect. BA's competitors have not fared so well, although load factors on these routes are mostly quite close to the airlines own average. (Dan Air to Manchester is the glaring exception, and the route is now no longer flown.)

64.   Without making comparisons with the individual results of other routes (for which information is not available) it is impossible to say much more about the impact of liberalisation on load factors. However, it is clear from the data that is available that competition on the domestic trunks has not resulted in a dramatic decline in load factors on those routes, and nor has liberalisation in the rest of the market produced an overall steep decline.

Effect on airlines

65.   Disagregated financial data for airline operation which enables one to separate out the scheduled domestic operations is not available. Financial data for airlines includes any charter and international scheduled operations that they may undertake. As the costs of these different sorts of operation are different, changes in the balance between them will have an effect on the financial performance of the airline. In addition, domestic scheduled operations may make up only a small proportion of the airlines output. Thus, changes in this field of operation will only have a small effect on the published figures.

66.   This problem is particularly acute with British Airways, as its domestic operations account for only a small proportion of its total (in the order of 10 per cent of aircraft km in 1984). In addition, British Airways has been radically reorganised in the 1981-86 time period in order for it to be privatised. This will be likely to swamp any effect resulting from the change in domestic regulation.

Table 17

BRITISH AIRWAYS DOMINANCE

(Seat Kilometers, millions)

	1976	1981	1986
Total Seat Km available.	3.8M	4.1M	5.9M
British Airways (% of total)	73	60	54
Air UK	2	6	4
British Caledonian	11	10	7
British Midland	8	14	18
Dan Air	2	6	8
Others	4	4	9

Source: CAA Annual Statistics.

160

67.   British Airway's dominance of the domestic market has declined considerably over the the period 1976-86. In the first time period (1976-81) BA's output actually declined, from 3.5 Million seat kms to 2.5M., rising again to 3.2M by 1986. BA withdrew from a considerable number of routes in the first period, to be replaced by other carriers. In the second period, at least on the domestic trunks, BA lost some of its market share on routes it continued to operate.

68.   British Caledonian also lost some of its market share over the ten year period. On the whole the airlines that were small in 1976 expanded, while the two larger ones contracted.

Airline personnel costs

69.   Table 17 gives the average salary of pilots for the smaller UK airlines as a percentage of average for BA's pilots. Although this gives a rather biased result, as BA's costs are dominated by pilots flying international routes, it does indicate that BA's pilots costs are rising faster than the other airlines.

Table 18

PILOTS AND CO-PILOTS COSTS, AS A % OF BA's COSTS

	1976	1981	1986
British Airways	100	100	100
Air UK	56	56	41
British Caledonian	103	103	78
British Midland	85	86	64
Dan Air	80	76	63

Source: CAA Annual Statistics.

Table 19

PILOTS AND CO-PILOTS COSTS INDEXED (BA IN 1976=100)
AND DEFLATED BY THE RPI

	1976	1981	1986
British Airways	100	116	162
Air UK	56	65	66
British Caledonian	103	119	126
British Midland	85	100	104
Dan Air	80	88	102

Source: CAA Annual Statistics.

70. All the airlines except BA show real increases in cost of around 20-25 per cent over the ten year period. In comparison BA's cost increase by 62 per cent. Given that BA starts off with costs higher than the other airlines (except BCal) BA would appear to be becoming less competitive over time, at least on this measure.

71. It is also interesting that for airlines other than British Airways the real increase in pilot costs slows down in the second period, at the same time as some forms of price competition are beginning to emerge.

COMPETITION AND DEREGULATION OF THE UK DOMESTIC MARKET: CONCLUSIONS

72. The UK domestic market is still a long way from being fully competitive. CAA regulations on route licencing mean that for the majority of routes an airline that is performing reasonably well will be protected from the threat of substitution. For routes that may sustain two (or more) carriers limited forms of price competition may be possible under the terms of the regulations. However, the number of routes that can sustain two (or more) airlines is limited, and is further constrained by congestion problems at London Heathrow (and possibly Gatwick) -- see below.

73. The impact of deregulation on normal prices does not seem to be very significant. If there is an effect on prices it is a one off (relative) reduction in the economy price at the time of entry of a new carrier. Longer term price competition seems to be confined to discount fares.

74. The market in discount fares has changed considerably over the last 10 years. There is some evidence to suggest that some of the impetus for the development of these fares has come from competition between airlines. (Although a profit maximising monopolist may also find it rational to segment the market in this way.)

75. The majority of the growth of the domestic market has come from expansion in the discount market. The price of full price tickets has increased faster than the RPI, while the price of cheapest discount tickets has tended to reduce relative to full price tickets. As the number of types of discount tickets available has increased the average price paid by passengers is likely to have decreased, (relative to full price tickets), even faster.

76. British Airways dominance of the domestic market has been considerably reduced. In the first instance by the withdrawl of British Airways from some domestic routes and, more recently, by the reduction of BA's market share on competitive routes.

77. At least in some areas British Airway's costs are still increasing faster than other domestic airlines and have, in general, been higher to begin with. However, without data on the costs of BA's domestic operations it is impossible to say whether, overall, BA is more or less competitive than the other airlines or whether it is getting more or less competitive.

78.   For regulatory purposes it is important to get a more definitive answer to this question because if British Airways is less competitive than the other airlines, or is getting less competitive, it would suggest that structural cross-subsidy is being used to maintain its domestic output.

79.   The partial relaxation of entry onto existing routes in the early 80's seems to have expanded airline output by increasing traffic on existing routes. When route entry was confined to opening up new routes expansion of output seems to have been channeled in this direction. This would suggest that competition on a single route, even when tightly constrained, tends to increase total output.

80.   Overall, partial competition does not seem to have led to significant reductions in load factors, although there is some evidence that competition leads to a faster increase in frequency of service, (which must be partially balanced by a reduction in the size of plane used). However, without detailed data on load factors for individual routes it is impossible to check how far this is true outside of the domestic trunk routes.

81.   Overall, partial deregulation seems to have been a success. However, the main impetus to improvement seems to come from the actual entry of a new airline on a route. The number of routes left where this can take place in the near future is limited. Therefore, there must be some doubt about gaining further benefit unless the rules on airline substitution are changed. In addition, the continued dominance of British Airways in a market where its relative competitiveness is unknown, where its ability to cross-subsidise is considerable and where it is only lightly constrained from meeting any price competition, must cast some doubt on the future willingness of smaller airlines to compete on price even if this is a reflection of a genuine cost advantage.

Interaction with airports policy

82.   UK domestic deregulation comes up against airports policy in relation to access to Heathrow (and, to a much lesser extent, Gatwick). There are two aspects to this problem, the slot problem and the international hub problem.

83.   Heathrow is effectively running at maximum capacity at present. In response to this no new domestic services are to be licensed to fly into Heathrow unless there is an overwhelming 'public interest' case. In terms of airline competition, this has the important result that routes from Heathrow are effectively protected from additional airline entry, no matter how dense the route becomes.

84.   In addition, no new UK airline is allowed to fly international routes out of Heathrow. As most UK domestic carriers are also international airlines this stops them forming a hub at Heathrow to link their domestic and international routes, even if they could get (or have) permission to fly domestic routes into Heathrow. In so far as airlines enjoy economies of scale in developing a hub and spoke networks this can put new entrant airlines at a competitive disadvantage.

85.   One additional point needs to be made in relation to capacity constrained airports. Under the usual arrangements for slot allocation airlines have de facto ownership of slots. An airline with a large number of slots has a considerable freedom to manipulate his timetable to secure short term competitive gains (e.g. by sandwiching a competitors flight). A new entrant airline may be unable to fight back against this type of behaviour, and will be forced to leave the market.

86.   Unless the allocation of access to capacity constrained airports is reformed so as to facilitate competition in the domestic market it will continue to act as a significant brake on the deregulation process.

87.   Limitation of airport capacity and access to slots is one of the major factors to be taken into account in assessing the recent merger proposal (July 1987) between British Airways and British Caledonian.   British Airways currently occupies approximately 40 per cent of all occupied slots at Heathrow the next biggest user being British Midland with around 10 per cent.   At Gatwick, where runway capacity is a constraint in peak times, British Airways has about 10 per cent of occupied slots and British Caledonian about 20 per cent.   Thus, the merger would result in dominance of the merged airline in Gatwick while it continues to be dominant at Heathrow.

Implications for international liberalisation

88.   Most of the conclusions above are relevant to the debate on international liberalisation. It is, however, worth stressing one of the conclusions again, and that is that the major effects of the liberalisation process seem to come from the actual entry of new carriers, not from competition between existing carriers when they are protected from either substitution or additional competition.   Therefore, most of the reform packages currently being discussed in Europe are likely to have only a limited impact, as the areas where there will be free entry are either restricted (the EEC package) or virtually non-existent (the ECAC proposals).

20 PER CENT SAMPLE

Table 2A

ECONOMY FARES

	1976 £	1981 £	% Change	1986 £	% Change	% Change 76-86
20 PER CENT SAMPLE OF UK DOMESTIC ROUTES						
Aberdeen Birmingham	32.90	67.00	104	84.00	25	155
Barra Glasgow	19.30	33.00	71	50.50	53	162
Belfast Bristol	25.90	55.00	112	75.00	36	189
Belfast East Mid.	21.40	43.00	101	69.00	60	222
Belfast Exeter	25.90	50.00	93	82.00	64	216
Belfast Glasgow	12.80	32.50	154	47.66	47	272
Belfast IOM	10.90	28.00	157	39.00	39	257
Belfast Leeds	18.90	43.50	130	55.00	26	191
Belfast London (G)	25.00	39.00	56	65.00	67	160
Belfast Manchester	17.30	40.00	131	55.75	39	222
Birmingham Manchester	9.20	17.50	90	31.00	77	236
Blackpool Jersey	24.20	52.00	115	80.00	54	231
Bournemouth Guernsey	13.30	28.50	114	37.50	32	181
Bournemouth Jersey	13.30	28.50	114	37.50	32	181
East Mid. Guernsey	20.80	42.50	104	68.00	60	226
Eday Kirkwall	5.40	11.00	104	16.30	48	202
Fetlar Whalsay	4.60	6.00	30	8.20	37	78
Glasgow IOM	12.60	29.00	130	45.00	55	257
Glasgow London (G)	24.00	56.00	133	70.00	25	192
Glasgow Manchester	19.10	41.00	115	56.50	38	196
Glasgow Tiree	14.40	26.00	80	38.50	48	167
Glasgow Stornoway	24.10	49.50	105	65.00	31	169
Inverness Lerwick	22.00	49.00	123	69.00	41	213
IOM London (H)	20.20	46.00	128	65.00	41	222
Jersey Plymouth	13.50	33.50	148	45.00	34	233
Kirkwall Lerwick	11.30	27.00	139	34.50	28	205
Kirkwall N. Ronaldsay	5.40	11.00	104	16.30	48	202
Kirkwall Stronsay	5.40	11.00	104	16.30	48	202
London (H) Manchester	18.20	38.00	109	53.00	39	191
Norwich Teeside	19.30	45.00	133	57.00	27	195

Table 5A

LOWEST DISCOUNT FARE AS A PERCENTAGE OF THE ECONOMY FARE

	1976	1981	1986
20 PER CENT SAMPLE OF UK DOMESTIC ROUTES			
Aberdeen Birmingham	100	49	38
Barra Glasgow	80	67	66
Belfast Bristol	100	64	63
Belfast East Mid.	100	67	64
Belfast Exeter	100	50	100
Belfast Glasgow	100	68	59
Belfast IOM	100	63	67
Belfast Leeds	100	51	77
Belfast London (G)	64	64	34
Belfast Manchester	100	71	43
Birmingham Manchester	61	100	43
Blackpool Jersey	100	50	100
Bournemouth Guernsey	62	70	73
Bournemouth Jersey	62	70	73
East Mid. Guernsey	61	62	66
Eday Kirkwall	89	81	82
Fetlar Whalsay	100	100	100
Glasgow IOM	100	50	81
Glasgow London (G)	75	45	49
Glasgow Manchester	50	50	38
Glasgow Tiree	100	65	68
Glasgow Stornoway	100	67	57
Inverness Lerwick	100	59	54
IOM London (H)	88	65	68
Jersey Plymouth	62	32	81
Kirkwall Lerwick	100	65	67
Kirkwall N. Ronaldsay	100	81	83
Kirkwall Stronsay	100	81	83
London (H) Manchester	100	53	52
Norwich Teeside	100	50	51
AVERAGE (All fares)	89	62	66
AVERAGE (Discount fares)	69	62	66

Table 6A

NUMBER OF DIFFERENT TYPES OF DISCOUNT TICKETS AVAILABLE PER ROUTE

	1976	1981	1986
PER CENT SAMPLE OF UK DOMESTIC ROUTES			
Aberdeen Birmingham	0	1	4
Barra Glasgow	1	1	2
Belfast Bristol	0	2	2
Belfast East Mid.	0	3	4
Belfast Exeter	0	4	0
Belfast Glasgow	0	2	6
Belfast IOM	0	4	5
Belfast Leeds	0	4	2
Belfast London (G)	1	2	6
Belfast Manchester	0	1	7
Birmingham Manchester	1	0	1
Blackpool Jersey	0	4	0
Bournemouth Guernsey	1	3	7
Bournemouth Jersey	1	3	7
East Mid. Guernsey	1	5	2
Eday Kirkwall	1	1	1
Fetlar Whalsay	0	0	0
Glasgow IOM	0	4	2
Glasgow London (G)	1	3	6
Glasgow Manchester	1	1	8
Glasgow Tiree	0	1	1
Glasgow Stornoway	0	2	3
Inverness Lerwick	0	1	3
IOM London (H)	1	4	3
Jersey Plymouth	1	2	3
Kirkwall Lerwick	0	2	3
Kirkwall N. Ronaldsay	0	1	1
Kirkwall Stronsay	0	1	1
London (H) Manchester	0	3	4
Norwich Teeside	0	3	2
AVERAGE	0.34	2.2	3.1

NOTES AND REFERENCES

1.   Civil Aviation Act, 1971 HMSO, London, 1971, section 3(1)(a).

2.   Ibid, section 3(1)(d).

3.   Ibid, section 3(3).

4.   Civil aviation policy guidance, Cmnd 4899, 1972.

5.   Future civil aviation policy, Cmnd 6400, 1976.

6.   Ibid, part II, para 9 and Civil aviation policy guidance, op. cit, para 16.

7.   Future of civil aviation policy, op. cit, Part II, paras 2,3 and 9.

8.   CAA, official record series 2, No.207, part 4.2, March 1976.

9.   Ibid, para 2.

10.   Ibid, para 5.

11.   CAA, official record series 2, No.393, part 4.2, 27th November 1979. There was a reissue of the criteria for licensing new short haul routes in 1978 which were virtually identical to the 1976 ones.

12.   Ibid, para 2.

13.   Ibid, para 5.

14.   CAA. CAP 420, Domestic air services, 1979.

15.   CAA official record series 2, No.465, part 4.2, 28th April 1981. Also published as CAP 444, statement of policies on air transport licensing, CAA, 1981.

16.   Ibid, para 8.

17.   Ibid, para 9.

18.   Ibid, para 14.

19.   CAA, Consultation on airline competition policy: an interim assessment, CAP 489, 1984.

20.   CAA, Airline competition policy, CAP 500, 1984.

21.   Ibid, para 101.

22.   CAA official record series 2, 8th Jan 1985. Also published as CAP 501, Statement of policies on air transport licensing, Jan 1985.

23.   CAA, Decision on air transport licence application, 12/85, July 1985.

24.   CAA, Decision on air transport licence application, 13/85, July 1985.

25.   Future civil aviation policy, op. cit, para 16.

26.   CAA, official record series 2, No.465, part 4.2, para 19.

27.   CAP 501, op. cit, para 15.

28.   ABC World Airways Guide, May, 1986.

29.   Ibid, and May 1981 and May 1976.

30.   CAA, Competition on the main domestic trunk routes, CAA paper 87005, March 1987. para 2.1.

31.   Ibid, para 14.4.

20.   CAA, Airline competition policy, CAP 500, 1984.

21.   ibid, para 101.

22.   CAA official record series 2, 6th Jan 1985. Also published as CAP 501, Statement of policies on air transport licensing, Jan 1985.

23.   CAA, Decision on air transport licence application, 18/85, July 1985

24.   CAA, Decision on air transport licence application, 13/85, July 1985.

25.   Future civil aviation policy, op. cit, para 16.

26.   CAA, official record series 2, No.955, part 4.2, para 19

27.   CAP 501, op. cit, para 16.

28.   ABC World Airways Guide, May 1986.

29.   ibid and May 1981 and May 1975.

30.   CAA, Competition on the major domestic trunk routes, CAA paper 87005, March 1987, para 2.1

31.   ibid, para 14.4.

WHERE TO OBTAIN OECD PUBLICATIONS
OÙ OBTENIR LES PUBLICATIONS DE L'OCDE

ARGENTINA - ARGENTINE
Carlos Hirsch S.R.L.,
Florida 165, 4º Piso,
(Galeria Guemes) 1333 Buenos Aires
Tel. 33.1787.2391 y 30.7122

AUSTRALIA - AUSTRALIE
D.A. Book (Aust.) Pty. Ltd.
11-13 Station Street (P.O. Box 163)
Mitcham, Vic. 3132   Tel. (03) 873 4411

AUSTRIA - AUTRICHE
OECD Publications and Information Centre,
4 Simrockstrasse,
5300 Bonn (Germany)   Tel. (0228) 21.60.45
Gerold & Co., Graben 31, Wien 1 Tel. 52.22.35

BELGIUM - BELGIQUE
Jean de Lannoy,
Avenue du Roi 202
B-1060 Bruxelles   Tel. (02) 538.51.69

CANADA
Renouf Publishing Company Ltd/
Éditions Renouf Ltée,
1294 Algoma Road, Ottawa, Ont. K1B 3W8
Tel. (613) 741-4333
Toll Free/Sans Frais:
Ontario, Quebec, Maritimes:
1-800-267-1805
Western Canada, Newfoundland:
1-800-267-1826
Stores/Magasins:
61 rue Sparks St., Ottawa, Ont. K1P 5A6
Tel: (613) 238-8985
211 rue Yonge St., Toronto, Ont. M5B 1M4
Tel: (416) 363-3171
Federal Publications Inc.,
301-303 King St. W.,
Toronto, Ont. M5V 1J5
Tel. (416)581-1552
Les Éditions la Liberté inc.,
3020 Chemin Sainte-Foy,
Sainte-Foy, P.Q. G1X 3V6,
Tel. (418)658-3763

DENMARK - DANEMARK
Munksgaard Export and Subscription Service
35, Nørre Søgade, DK-1370 København K
Tel. +45.1.12.85.70

FINLAND - FINLANDE
Akateeminen Kirjakauppa,
Keskuskatu 1, 00100 Helsinki 10   Tel. 0.12141

FRANCE
OCDE/OECD
Mail Orders/Commandes par correspondance :
2, rue André-Pascal,
75775 Paris Cedex 16
Tel. (1) 45.24.82.00
Bookshop/Librairie : 33, rue Octave-Feuillet
75016 Paris
Tel. (1) 45.24.81.67 or/ou (1) 45.24.81.81
Librairie de l'Université,
12a, rue Nazareth,
13602 Aix-en-Provence   Tel. 42.26.18.08

GERMANY - ALLEMAGNE
OECD Publications and Information Centre,
4 Simrockstrasse,
5300 Bonn   Tel. (0228) 21.60.45

GREECE - GRÈCE
Librairie Kauffmann,
28, rue du Stade, 105 64 Athens Tel. 322.21.60

HONG KONG
Government Information Services,
Publications (Sales) Office,
Information Services Department
No. 1, Battery Path, Central

ICELAND - ISLANDE
Snæbjörn Jónsson & Co., h.f.,
Hafnarstræti 4 & 9,
P.O.B. 1131 - Reykjavik
Tel. 13133/14281/11936

INDIA - INDE
Oxford Book and Stationery Co.,
Scindia House, New Delhi 110001
Tel. 331.5896/5308
17 Park St., Calcutta 700016   Tel. 240832

INDONESIA - INDONÉSIE
Pdii-Lipi, P.O. Box 3065/JKT.Jakarta
Tel. 583467

IRELAND - IRLANDE
TDC Publishers - Library Suppliers,
12 North Frederick Street, Dublin 1
Tel. 744835-749677

ITALY - ITALIE
Libreria Commissionaria Sansoni,
Via Lamarmora 45, 50121 Firenze
Tel. 579751/584468
Via Bartolini 29, 20155 Milano   Tel. 365083
La diffusione delle pubblicazioni OCSE viene
assicurata dalle principali librerie ed anche da :
Editrice e Libreria Herder,
Piazza Montecitorio 120, 00186 Roma
Tel. 6794628
Libreria Hœpli,
Via Hœpli 5, 20121 Milano   Tel. 865446
Libreria Scientifica
Dott. Lucio de Biasio "Aeiou"
Via Meravigli 16, 20123 Milano   Tel. 807679

JAPAN - JAPON
OECD Publications and Information Centre,
Landic Akasaka Bldg., 2-3-4 Akasaka,
Minato-ku, Tokyo 107   Tel. 586.2016

KOREA - CORÉE
Kyobo Book Centre Co. Ltd.
P.O.Box: Kwang Hwa Moon 1658,
Seoul   Tel. (REP) 730.78.91

LEBANON - LIBAN
Documenta Scientifica/Redico,
Edison Building, Bliss St.,
P.O.B. 5641, Beirut   Tel. 354429-344425

MALAYSIA/SINGAPORE -
MALAISIE/SINGAPOUR
University of Malaya Co-operative Bookshop
Ltd.,
7 Lrg 51A/227A, Petaling Jaya
Malaysia   Tel. 7565000/7565425
Information Publications Pte Ltd
Pei-Fu Industrial Building,
24 New Industrial Road No. 02-06
Singapore 1953   Tel. 2831786, 2831798

NETHERLANDS - PAYS-BAS
SDU Uitgeverij
Christoffel Plantijnstraat 2
Postbus 20014
2500 EA's-Gravenhage   Tel. 070-789911
Voor bestellingen: Tel. 070-789880

NEW ZEALAND - NOUVELLE-ZÉLANDE
Government Printing Office Bookshops:
Auckland: Retail Bookshop, 25 Rutland Stseet,
Mail Orders, 85 Beach Road
Private Bag C.P.O.
Hamilton: Retail: Ward Street,
Mail Orders, P.O. Box 857
Wellington: Retail, Mulgrave Street, (Head
Office)
Cubacade World Trade Centre,
Mail Orders, Private Bag
Christchurch: Retail, 159 Hereford Street,
Mail Orders, Private Bag
Dunedin: Retail, Princes Street,
Mail Orders, P.O. Box 1104

NORWAY - NORVÈGE
Tanum-Karl Johan
Karl Johans gate 43, Oslo 1
PB 1177 Sentrum, 0107 Oslo 1Tel. (02) 42.93.10

PAKISTAN
Mirza Book Agency
65 Shahrah Quaid-E-Azam, Lahore 3 Tel. 66839

PHILIPPINES
I.J. Sagun Enterprises, Inc.
P.O. Box 4322 CPO Manila
Tel. 695-1946, 922-9495

PORTUGAL
Livraria Portugal,
Rua do Carmo 70-74,
1117 Lisboa Codex   Tel. 360582/3

SINGAPORE/MALAYSIA -
SINGAPOUR/MALAISIE
See "Malaysia/Singapor". Voir
« Malaisie/Singapour »

SPAIN - ESPAGNE
Mundi-Prensa Libros, S.A.,
Castelló 37, Apartado 1223, Madrid-28001
Tel. 431.33.99
Libreria Bosch, Ronda Universidad 11,
Barcelona 7   Tel. 317.53.08/317.53.58

SWEDEN - SUÈDE
AB CE Fritzes Kungl. Hovbokhandel,
Box 16356, S 103 27 STH,
Regeringsgatan 12,
DS Stockholm   Tel. (08) 23.89.00
Subscription Agency/Abonnements:
Wennergren-Williams AB,
Box 30004, S104 25 Stockholm Tel. (08)54.12.00

SWITZERLAND - SUISSE
OECD Publications and Information Centre,
4 Simrockstrasse,
5300 Bonn (Germany)   Tel. (0228) 21.60.45
Librairie Payot,
6 rue Grenus, 1211 Genève 11
Tel. (022) 31.89.50
United Nations Bookshop/Librairie des Nations-
Unies
Palais des Nations,
1211 - Geneva 10
Tel. 022-34-60-11 (ext. 48 72)

TAIWAN - FORMOSE
Good Faith Worldwide Int'l Co., Ltd.
9th floor, No. 118, Sec.2
Chung Hsiao E. Road
Taipei   Tel. 391.7396/391.7397

THAILAND - THAILANDE
Suksit Siam Co., Ltd., 1715 Rama IV Rd.,
Samyam Bangkok 5   Tel. 2511630
INDEX Book Promotion & Service Ltd.
59/6 Soi Lang Suan, Ploenchit Road
Patjumamwan, Bangkok 10500
Tel. 250-1919, 252-1066

TURKEY - TURQUIE
Kültur Yayinlari Is-Türk Ltd. Sti.
Atatürk Bulvari No: 191/Kat. 21
Kavaklidere/Ankara   Tel. 25.07.60
Dolmabahce Cad. No: 29
Besiktas/Istanbul   Tel. 160.71.88

UNITED KINGDOM - ROYAUME-UNI
H.M. Stationery Office,
Postal orders only: (01)211-5656
P.O.B. 276, London SW8 5DT
Telephone orders: (01) 622.3316, or
Personal callers:
49 High Holborn, London WC1V 6HB
Branches at: Belfast, Birmingham,
Bristol, Edinburgh, Manchester

UNITED STATES - ÉTATS-UNIS
OECD Publications and Information Centre,
2001 L Street, N.W., Suite 700,
Washington, D.C. 20036 - 4095
Tel. (202) 785.6323

VENEZUELA
Libreria del Este,
Avda F. Miranda 52, Aptdo. 60337,
Edificio Galipan, Caracas 106
Tel. 951.17.05/951.23.07/951.12.97

YUGOSLAVIA - YOUGOSLAVIE
Jugoslovenska Knjiga, Knez Mihajlova 2,
P.O.B. 36, Beograd   Tel. 621.992

Orders and inquiries from countries where
Distributors have not yet been appointed should be
sent to:
OECD, Publications Service, 2, rue André-Pascal,
75775 PARIS CEDEX 16.

Les commandes provenant de pays où l'OCDE n'a
pas encore désigné de distributeur doivent être
adressées à :
OCDE, Service des Publications. 2, rue André-
Pascal, 75775 PARIS CEDEX 16.

71784-05-1988

OECD PUBLICATIONS, 2, rue André-Pascal, 75775 PARIS CEDEX 16 - No. 44423 1988
PRINTED IN FRANCE
(24 88 02 1) ISBN 92-64-13101-9